Amélie

CINÉ-FILES: The French Film Guides
Series Editor: Ginette Vincendeau

From the pioneering days of the Lumière brothers' Cinématographe in 1895, France has been home to perhaps the most consistently vibrant film culture in the world, producing world-class directors and stars, and a stream of remarkable movies, from popular genre films to cult avant-garde works. Many of these have found a devoted audience outside France, and the arrival of DVD is now enabling a whole new generation to have access to contemporary titles as well as the great classics of the past.

The Ciné-Files French Film Guides build on this welcome new access, offering authoritative and entertaining guides to some of the most significant titles, from the silent era to the early twenty-first century. Written by experts in French cinema, the books combine extensive research with the author's distinctive, sometimes provocative perspective on each film. The series will thus build up an essential collection on great French classics, enabling students, teachers and lovers of French cinema both to learn more about their favourite films and make new discoveries in one of the world's richest bodies of cinematic work.

Ginette Vincendeau

Published Ciné-Files
Alphaville (Jean-Luc Godard, 1965) – Chris Darke
Les Diaboliques (Henri-Georges Clouzot, 1955) – Susan Hayward
La Haine (Mathieu Kassovitz, 1995) – Ginette Vincendeau
La Reine Margot (Patrice Chéreau, 1994) – Julianne Pidduck

Forthcoming Ciné-Files include:
Amélie (Jean-Pierre Jeunet, 2001) – Isabelle Vanderschelden
Le Corbeau (Henri-Georges Clouzot, 1943) – Judith Mayne
Casque d'or (Jacques Becker, 1952) – Sarah Leahy
Cléo de 5 à 7 (Agnès Varda, 1961) – Valerie Orpen
La Règle du jeu (Jean Renoir, 1939) – Keith Reader
Rififi (Jules Dassin, 1955) – Alastair Phillips
La Grande illusion (Jean Renoir, 1937) – Martin O'Shaughnessy
Un chien andalou (Luis Buñuel, 1929) – Elza Adamowicz
À bout de souffle (Jean-Luc Godard, 1960) – Ramona Fotiade

Amélie

Le Fabuleux destin d'
Amélie Poulain

(Jean-Pierre Jeunet, 2001)

Isabelle Vanderschelden

I.B. TAURIS

LONDON · NEW YORK

Reprinted in 2010 by I.B.Tauris & Co. Ltd

6 Salem Road, London W2 4BU

175 Fifth Avenue, New York NY 10010

ibtauris.com

First Published in 2007 by I.B.Tauris & Co. Ltd

ISBN: 978 1 84511 375 9

A full CIP record for this book is available from the British Library

Typeset in Minion by Dexter Haven Associates Ltd, London
Printed and bound in India by Replika Press Pvt. Ltd.

Contents

Note and acknowledgements

All film references and titles are given in French and English. For convenience I have adopted the shorter English-language title *Amelie* to refer to *Le Fabuleux destin d'Amélie Poulain*. For all the other films I used the original title after the first mention. All the statistical and box office information provided in this book comes from the CNC and the IMDb database unless otherwise indicated. References are given in footnotes in full, except when the work is in bibliography. All French quotations are my own translations, unless otherwise indicated.

I would like to thank the Department of Languages and my colleagues at Manchester Metropolitan University for their support and encouragement, the British Academy for funding two research trips to Paris, as well as the BIFI and CNC libraries and their friendly staff.

My thanks also go to Patricia Allmer, David Bellos, Philippa Brewster, Rachida Chekaf, Bruno Delbonnel, Barbara Lebrun, Barbara and Emilie Lehin, Phil Powrie, Darren Waldron for their suggestions, and to Valérie Orpen, Anne Wright and Gordon Eccleston for reading the draft versions. Above all, I am grateful to Ginette Vincendeau for offering me the chance to write this book, and for her support as editor.

Synopsis

Amelie starts with a narrated prologue that retraces the life of the main character. Born near Paris in 1973, Amélie Poulain is the only child of eccentric parents, a taciturn doctor who thought she had a heart defect because she got excited when he checked her pulse, and an overprotective mother who died in a freak accident when her daughter was still a child. Amélie had a sheltered upbringing, and she compensated for her loneliness by creating her own world and friends through her vivid imagination.

In 1997, Amélie, now an adult, lives alone in a small flat in Montmartre, and works in a local café, *Les Deux Moulins*. Still seeing the world through the eyes of a child, she relishes the small pleasures of everyday life and she regularly visits her father in the suburbs. One evening, as she has just learnt about Princess Diana's death, she accidentally finds an old box full of a child's treasures that had been concealed in her bathroom wall in the 1950s. She sets out to find its owner (a man now in his forties named Bretodeau) in order to return the box. Her investigation gives her the opportunity to meet her neighbours, including a painter suffering from a rare bone disease, Raymond Dufayel, and the concierge, Madeleine Wallace. She realises that they all seem to have some problem that makes their lives unhappy.

Having returned the box to its owner and seeing the extraordinary effect that it had, she decides to give her life some purpose by devoting herself to helping people around her, bringing them a little happiness anonymously. Her first tasks include cheering up a blind man and avenging simple-minded assistant Lucien who is bullied by his boss, the grocer Collignon. Then, she helps her hypochondriac colleague Georgette to find a soulmate (temporarily). She brings back a smile to the concierge's face by sending her a fake love letter from her (late) husband pretending that it had been lost in the post. By the end of the film she has even surreptitiously convinced her father to realise his lifelong dream of travelling the world.

However, Amélie is increasingly distracted in her missions, as in her incessant trips round Paris she has met a strange young man, Nino Quincampoix, who works in a sex shop and collects the old passport photographs discarded in automatic photo booths around the City. Nino is obsessed by the image of a bald man with red shoes whose identity is a mystery. In many ways Nino is like Amélie, lonely and eccentric. She falls in love with him instantly, starts looking for him but, having located him, is too shy to approach him directly. Instead, she devises a series of convoluted plans including treasure hunts and games of hide-and-seek. She makes mysterious telephone calls, adopts disguises and sends cryptic messages.

When she discovers by chance the secret of the mystery man with the red shoes, Amélie still cannot bring herself to meet Nino face to face, possibly because she is afraid of confronting reality. A first date in the café fails to materialise, but Nino will eventually track her down at her flat. With a little help from the painter, they finally embark on romance.

Introduction

Twenty-fifth April 2001. *Le Fabuleux destin d'Amélie Poulain/Amelie* is released in French cinemas. It is Jean-Pierre Jeunet's fourth feature film, after successful collaborations with Marc Caro in the 1990s for *Delicatessen* (1991) and *La Cité des enfants perdus/The City of Lost Children* (1995), and a solo incursion into Hollywood to direct *Alien: Resurrection* (1998).

October 2004. Jeunet's fifth film, *Un long dimanche de fiançailles/A Very Long Engagement*, is about to be released and many reviews, including this one published in *Le Point*, start with a reference to *Amelie*:

> May 2001: there is only one name on the lips of eight million French people and that is Amélie. Their hearts are light and they believe again in happiness, in Montmartre and in poetic realism. *Amelie* is everywhere, Audrey Tautou has become the fiancée of French people, and the film smashes all records of popularity in the USA. What a fabulous adventure for a pretty and unpretentious film, that bears the signature of Jean-Pierre Jeunet who, till then, had only been associated with the margins of popular cinema making fantasy films, with a touch of the fantastic.[1]

In the context of French cinema, 2001 was the year of *Amelie*. In future years, anything that Jeunet may do will be compared to *Amelie*, because the film and its eponymous heroine have left a lasting impression in the collective memory. Another indication of the impact of the film is the number of cinema books and year retrospectives that chose to put Amélie's face on their covers.[2] The Amélie in question, a shy and lonely doe-eyed young woman with a quirky smile, works as a waitress in the Montmartre area of Paris, until one day she decides to devote herself to repairing the lives of the people around her. 'She's going to change your life', the film's poster promised. She certainly did change two lives significantly, those of director Jean-Pierre Jeunet and of the promising young actress Audrey Tautou.

Amelie was planned as a modest, personal film, designed to make people feel happy, but unlikely to become a box office hit. Becoming an instant success and a phenomenon, it was seen by 8.85 million viewers in France,[3] and around 30 million worldwide, which translates into overall receipts exceeding $100 million. It earned a positive critical reception, although it also created fierce controversy in some quarters. Winner of several César awards and prestigious international prizes, it was nominated for five Academy awards including Best Foreign Film.

According to the numerous reactions in the press and discussion websites, the viewers were touched by the film's optimistic set of values, its retro atmosphere, consensual themes and playful tone. It successfully blended romantic comedy and poetic realism, and it was praised for its stylish cinematography, making daring use of colour and special effects. These elements, combined with an evocative soundtrack, contributed to produce a popular film of universal appeal, encompassing most age groups and social backgrounds. Subsequently, *Amelie* was appropriated by the political sphere in a crucial electoral period, and gave rise to a critical controversy in the French media on the grounds that its artificiality and optimism offered a sanitised vision of France. After only a few years, *Amelie* is already established as a key film of the 2000s, an international emblem for French cinema, likely to become a popular classic.[4]

The first objective of this book is to situate *Amelie* within the context of the French film industry. Chapter One looks at Jeunet's career in film up to *Amelie* and briefly contextualises the national French film industry in 2001, a year often classed as exceptional. It explores the genesis of the film and introduces the production team, including the technical crew and cast. The next chapter provides an in-depth analysis of the film, drawing upon narrative strategies, genre, characterisation and gender perspectives. Chapter Three continues this by examining Jeunet's distinctive signature, a mixture of perfectionist composition and fertile imagination. More particularly it discusses the use of sound, colour, state-of-the-art special effects and digital postproduction.

The final chapter explores the reception of the film at home and abroad. At a time when French cinema is often said to be going through important structural changes and a survival crisis, *Amelie* caught the imagination of the public and mobilised critical discourse. It also provided more evidence of the French 'cultural exception' in the wake of the controversy between France and the United States arising from the GATT Free Trade Agreements in the 1990s. In this respect, the phenomenal success of the film, and also the criticisms that it attracted, exemplify the contradictions and challenges facing French cinema in the twenty-first century. In an increasingly globalised market, *Amelie* shows that the French film industry can produce popular films made in French that claim a distinctive identity. Such films offer an alternative to Hollywood, while embracing certain strategies of production and marketing that undoubtedly contribute to their transnational appeal.

Notes

1   F.G. Lorrain, 'Le douloureux destin de Mathilde', *Le Point*, 21 October 2004, p.108.
2   See *L'Année du cinéma 2001*, CNC, *Bilan 2001* 283 (May 2002), *Nos films de toujours* (Paris: Larousse, 2002); *Chronique du cinéma* (Paris: Chronique, 2002); R. Lanzoni, *French*

Cinema: From its Beginnings to the Present (London: Continuum, 2002); D. Anzel, *Le Cinéma* (Paris: Essentiels Milan, 2004).

3   This refers to the number of viewers by 31 December 2001. The CNC lists 9.19 million in the 2002 results.

4   The film is ranked in 25th place on the IMDb list of 250 best films of all times. Website http://www.imdb.com/chart/top, accessed on 2 August 2005.

1   Production contexts

Amelie is my personal film, one I had dreamed about for a long time.
J.-P. Jeunet[1]

From *Delicatessen* to *Amelie*: Jeunet's identity quest

Following the success of *Amelie*, the tremendous public and media interest around Jean-Pierre Jeunet's *Un long dimanche de fiançailles* in 2004 confirmed him as a leading contemporary director. The dossier devoted to this film in the cinema journal *Positif* described Jeunet as 'the national film-maker who develops the richest visual world, combined with a technical mastery and artistic sense, which place him on the level of Tim Burton, or even Francis Ford Coppola'.[2] In five films, he has reached international status, and successfully imposed his cinematic style, and this reputation can be attributed to a large extent to the phenomenal impact of *Amelie* in 2001.

Jeunet was born in Roanne, France, in 1953 and he often points to his provincial origins. Unlike many young directors who emerged in the 1990s, he had no formal cinema training. Having left school at 17 to work for the French postal services, he came to live in Paris in the 1970s, and was first drawn to the world of animation and comics, studying animation techniques with the Cinémation Studios. At the Annecy Animation Festival in 1974, Jeunet met Marc Caro, who regularly contributed drawings to satirical comic publications. They soon joined forces to produce several critical essays on various cartoon artists.[3] The influence of comics and animation on Jeunet's cinema career should not be underestimated. *La bande dessinée*, the collective name given to the rich and varied French comic production, is an integral part of French popular culture, which has a significant readership reaching all age groups.[4] Comics are seen as a privileged vehicle for fantasy, and have proved inspirational for a number of contemporary film-makers, including Patrice Leconte, Luc Besson and Jean-Jacques Beineix. Moreover, they have provided a wide-ranging source of cult material for adaptation into potential popular cinema blockbusters.[5]

In the late 1970s, Jeunet and Caro made two short animation films, *L'Évasion/The Escape* (1978) and *Le Manège/The Merry-Go-Round* (1979), for which Jeunet staged the *mise-en-scène* for the 'creatures' and dark world imagined by Caro. The latter won a César for best short animation. For their third short, *Le Bunker de la dernière rafale/The Last Burst Bunker* (1981), a film inspired by Expressionist aesthetics and the Punk culture of the 1980s, Jeunet and Caro spent a year making model army characters and their costumes, down to the smallest details. The film received a number of prizes, and was screened in a Paris cinema for six years.

Subsequently, Jeunet worked alone for his next short film made in black and white and narrated in voiceover, *Pas de repos pour Billy Brakko/No Rest for Billy Brakko* (1983), which toured the festival circuit. While considering himself self-taught, he gained valuable directorial experience making these short films, and also by filming high-profile television commercials and music videos for popular French singers such as Julien Clerc and Etienne Daho in the 1980s.[6] In the meantime, he continued to write film and animation reviews for magazines such as *Fantasmagorie, Charlie mensuel* and *Fluide glacial.*[7]

In 1989, *Foutaises/Things I Like, Things I Don't Like*, a short film written and directed by Jeunet alone, received several prizes including the César for best short film. It anticipated some of the thematic and stylistic motifs of *Amelie*, particularly the characterisation by likes and dislikes, and the insertion of stock shots.

Delicatessen

In 1991, Jeunet and Caro released their first feature film, *Delicatessen*, a small-budget dark comedy (FF 24 m), which became an international success. Produced by Claudie Ossard, who initially qualified the project as 'nearly impossible to finance in France',[8] it was written and directed in complete collaboration, even though each partner took on specific responsibilities. Jeunet dealt with the *mise-en-scène* and directing, which included the cutting, framing, camera positioning and actor direction, Caro supervised the visual aspects and artistic direction, including the storyboard, costumes and sets. Gilles Adrien, a former criminologist, collaborated on the screenplay.

The shooting took place over 16 weeks, mostly in studio sets constructed in a former warehouse outside Paris, and only the last scene was shot outdoors. The film attracted over two million viewers in France, was well received in Europe, and grossed $1.7 m in the USA. It received various awards, including four Césars for Best First Film, Best Editing, Best Original Screenplay and Best Production Design. This success was all the more unexpected as *Delicatessen* was a modest first film, with no stars and a young team of technicians.

Delicatessen contains little violence and few action scenes as such. It portrays a post-apocalyptic Gothic world in a surreal atmosphere that owes a great deal to the quality of Darius Khondji's lighting, which creates monochromic golden and sepia tones enhancing the pseudo-1940s look of the film. The narrative is set in two distinct spaces: the surface world consisting of the Delicatessen building and its residents, and the underworld shot in the Paris water reservoirs, inhabited by the dissident Troglodists, a group of cartoon-like creatures inspired by the *Alien* films.[9] The building was designed by the well-known artist Jean Rabasse, who also created a model version and the 'trompe l'œil' stairs. It is inhabited by unusual-looking, marginal characters with strange names whose casting took a whole year: Louison, the circus clown (Dominique Pinon), the butcher-murderer (Jean-Claude Dreyfus), his musician short-sighted daughter Julie (Marie-Laure Dougnac), the toy-making Kube brothers (Rufus and Mathou), and so on.

The film boasts a profusion of striking visual effects. Its imagery is clearly influenced by animation and comics, featuring Laurel and Hardy and Tex Avery style gags, and the burlesque humour of Buster Keaton. It evokes a circus-like atmosphere, its main character being a clown. Playful surprises and visual gags abound, starting with the credits scene, which associates each member of the technical crew with an emblematic visual reference related to their function, an idea that will resurface in *Amelie*. Throughout the film, special emphasis is placed on incongruous but familiar old-fashioned objects, which pervade the sets and the narrative, such as the mechanical monkey, the musical saw, the mooing boxes or the stupidity detector. They are often used as the props for the cartoon-like gags that punctuate the narrative, such as the emblematic knife-in-head trick, the three-legged dance act, the teacups ballet and soap bubble scenes.

Delicatessen gave Jeunet and Caro the chance to experiment with special effects and innovative techniques such as motion control, using computer-operated cameras. They also explored complex editing strategies, to perfect the synchronisation between sound and movement, for example in the scene where Louison is painting the stairs, or when the sound of the violin piece needs to blend with that of the squeaking bed. These special effects were adopted more to satisfy their perfectionist sense of detail than to shun technical difficulty: for the flooding scene at the end, for example, they chose to shoot in real time without any special effects. Other shots were conjured in semi-amateur fashion, confirming their taste for ingenious tricks. For instance, the nightmare scene used mirrors to produce distorted visual effects, mainly because state-of-the-art American technology was not available in France at the time.

An international cult film of the 1990s, *Delicatessen* inaugurated Jeunet and Caro's distinctive working methods, combining an obsessive sense of detail with a taste for devising complex mechanisms. These include the convoluted suicide plans of one of the characters that bring to mind the inventions of American cartoonist Rube Goldberg. More importantly, the film introduced distinctive stylistic elements that prefigure the visual style of *Amelie*, such as the use of wide-angle lenses, which distort faces, high-angle shots and exaggerated sound effects, which will be explored in more detail in Chapter Three.

La Cité des enfants perdus

The success of *Delicatessen* facilitated the production of another project on which Jeunet and Caro had started working as early as 1981. *La Cité des enfants perdus/The City of Lost Children* (1995), a dark and poetic futuristic fable with a substantial budget of FF 90 m, was shot over a period of five months in the 4,000 square metres of the Arpajon Studios in the Paris suburb.

An ambitious production, the film re-created a dazzling 'retro-futuristic' world to produce a dark fable, combining various sets of references and influences. Like *Delicatessen*, *La Cité des enfants perdus* used artefacts reminiscent of the world of the circus, but also an eclectic visual imagery inspired by a wide range of references: Charles Laughton's *Night of the Hunter*, Jules Verne, Charles Dickens, Perrault's tales, the cinema of Marcel Carné and Jacques Prévert, and even a sense of artifice recalling the films of Georges Méliès. It was also influenced by modern comic-strip artists such as Enki Bilal and Jean-Claude Forrest.[10]

Set in a dark and menacing imaginary harbour, the film features an ageing scientist Krank (Daniel Emilfork) who kidnaps children with the help of six clones (all played by Dominique Pinon), to steal their dreams in an attempt to reclaim his youth. After a child called Denrée (Joseph Lucien) is abducted, his brother One (Ron Pearlman), a circus strongman, joins forces with Miette (Judith Vittet), the nine-year-old leader of a gang of orphans, to attack Krank and free Denrée.

La Cité des enfants perdus follows a convoluted narrative, and it brings to life a number of improbable but memorable characters. However, it remains primarily a visual feast that calls upon a high level of technical prowess: it required seven months of postproduction work to edit the 40,000 digital images and the 144 takes used to create 17 minutes of special effects.[11] Accounting for ten per cent of the total budget, these were realised by Pitof, the special effects expert of French company Duboi, who had started working with Jeunet and Caro on *Delicatessen*. He led the second special effects team on *Alien: Resurrection*, and only missed *Amelie* because he was making his directorial debut with *Vidocq*.

La Cité des enfants perdus opened the 1995 Cannes Film Festival as part of the Official Selection. It was subsequently released nationally on 17 May 1995 in 150 prints. It attracted 239,000 viewers in France in its first week, and a total of 1.2 million overall, which was regarded as disappointing in view of the important budget and the publicity generated by Cannes. The film also benefited from an extensive international distribution, without repeating the success of *Delicatessen*, especially in the USA, where its reception was hampered by an R certificate (16) 'for disturbing and grotesque images of violence and menace'.[12]

The critical reception was mixed and, if the film received substantial attention from the French popular magazines like *Studio Magazine* and *Première*, it failed to mobilise the quality press reviewers.[13] Although the original visual style and fantasy were acknowledged, with Jean Rabasse's extraordinary set designs, and costumes designed by Jean-Paul Gaultier, many reviewers deplored the lack of emotion and the weakness of the narrative. They felt that the film was reduced to a visual tour de force, a catalogue of ideas, while little use was made of the actors' potential in terms of characterisation and performance.

Nevertheless, *La Cité des enfants perdus* remains a landmark in French cinema for its ground-breaking technical innovation and its visual originality. It heralded a series of French films relying on spectacular visual styles to compete on the reserved ground of special effects traditionally occupied by Hollywood, and to attract younger audiences and international markets with varying degrees of success (see Tables 2 and 3 in Appendix 2). But, above all, *La Cité des enfants perdus* reaffirmed Jeunet and Caro's reputation as innovative and ambitious film-makers, which provided a platform for Jeunet's next venture, a trip to Hollywood.

Alien: Resurrection

If *Alien: Resurrection* (1998) did not produce Jeunet's most compelling film or his best personal memories, it represented a significant career move, not least because it marked his emancipation from Caro, who did not take a direct part in the project. One of few French directors to draw Hollywood's attention, Jeunet was commissioned by 20th Century Fox to direct the fourth episode of the *Alien* series, *Alien: Resurrection*, with an estimated budget of $70 m.[14] Jeunet came to Hollywood preceded by his reputation as a European visionary director, not merely as a gifted technician. As Elisabeth Ezra has noted, in the eyes of the trade and the critics, Jeunet was considered an outsider, mainly because the themes of *Alien: Resurrection* incorporated European intellectual stereotypes, especially as his original ideas moved away from the traditional formulae.[15] He also brought with him a technical team capable of putting these ideas into practice, the best example being Darius Khondji's stunning photography, his bold use of saturated colours and light contrasts, which highlighted the dark atmosphere of the film.

Jeunet referred to the shooting of the film as a difficult yet exciting experience, partly due to the constraints of the Hollywood production system, which is so different from European film-making.[16] He reported that he 'had to be tough to resist pressure', yet felt that he was given the opportunity to leave his signature on the film by lending his personal touch to every shot. For example, it was his idea to use characters' breath as identification to open doors, and he introduced new twists into the script, reflecting his artistic aspirations and some of his own personal motifs (wide-angle shots, taste for mechanical devices, clones and deformed creatures). In this respect, the spectacular underwater scene was mentioned by the cast and crew as a memorable challenge.

Alien: Resurrection had a relatively disappointing reception in the USA, earning around $47 m with 2,415 prints, but it was better received overseas, particularly in Europe, with overall returns estimated around $150 m.[17] The critical reception was also mixed. *Alien* (Ridley Scott, 1979) had played on off-screen terror, *Aliens* (James Cameron, 1986) on action, while *Aliens 3* (David Fincher, 1992) focused on the relationship between the alien and Ripley and was considered as an aesthetic and formal exercise. *Alien: Resurrection* was disappointing for many, possibly because the sequel potential had been exhausted. It tried too hard to combine the treatments and themes of the previous three films, and it had a weaker script.[18] Nevertheless, it allowed Jeunet to fulfil the Hollywood dream of many European film-makers, showing his ability to handle big-budget high-tech productions, while raising his international profile.

This brief survey of the three films made by Jeunet before *Amelie* reveals his progressive acquisition of a distinctive visual style, achieved through unusual working methods. It signals the emergence of a set of core principles, which will be fully exploited in *Amelie*. By contributing to a wide variety of tasks, as diverse as scriptwriting and storyboarding, actor direction, set design, framing, lighting and editing, Jeunet was involved in the main levels of film production. He thus implemented a centralised system of production that brought him closer to *auteurism* than could be expected from a director readily associated with popular cinema, and influenced by animation and popular culture, as well as production and marketing values associated with Hollywood. In three films, he gained invaluable hands-on experience in studio shooting and insight into new technologies, including special effects and digital postproduction. Finally, he established a philosophy of perfectionism derived from hard work, careful preparation and special attention to small details.

Amelie in the context of the French film industry

2001: an exceptional year

2001 was the year of *Amelie*, but it also proved an exceptional year for French cinema at the domestic box office, with 20 films attracting over a million viewers – against eight in 2000 (see Table 1 in Appendix 2). Not only did viewers go to the cinema more, but they embraced French films enthusiastically, confirming the traditional appeal of comedies, as well as more spectacular genre films and 'intimist' psychological dramas. A series of favourable circumstances and exceptional box office results led to a 41.5 per cent market share for French films in 2001, after exceeding 50 per cent early in the year.[19] Several of these French box office hits had successful international careers.

The year 2001 also marked the advent of new directors capable of attracting young audiences into cinemas, with high-budget productions which combined familiar character types or narratives, clearly defined genres, spectacular special effects and aggressive promotional campaigns. These included Christophe Gans, who directed the hit *Le Pacte des loups/Brotherhood of the Wolf*, Jean-Paul Salomé and Olivier Dahan, whose respective films *Belphégor, le Fantôme du Louvre* and *Le Petit Poucet* were relative successes, which did not quite fulfil expectations, but were nevertheless seen by more than one million viewers. As for Pitof's eagerly expected *Vidocq*, it was the first fully digital film, shot using high-definition cameras, and confirming French cinema's interest in new technologies and the spectacular, but it had a poor critical response and, to some extent, a disappointing popular reception, considering its prestigious cast and lavish production values.[20]

Amelie came out in April 2001, but, as early as January, *Screen International* had reported on a new 'taste for the spectacular' in French cinema.[21] At the end of February, *Libération* entitled its report on the César Ceremony 'The start of the year is exceptional', echoing the popular success of comedies such as *Le Placard/The Closet* (Francis Veber). Interviewed for the occasion, the emblematic figure of French cinema and Unifrance director, Daniel Toscan du Plantier, joined in the euphoric tone of the article, stating that French cinema was turned to the future, with a thriving number of first films, and bridges appearing between art cinema and more commercial films.[22] By the end of 2001, many retrospective accounts of the year in the press reported an exceptional year for French cinema, pointing to *Amelie* as one of the catalysts of the success of French films, a perception confirmed by the annual report of the *Centre National de la Cinématographie* (CNC) in May 2002. Jeunet's film soon came to symbolise a turning point in the French film industry after the disappointing results of the previous years.

A number of other events in 2001 may have affected the reception of *Amelie*. The first reality TV show, *Loft Story*, the French equivalent of *Big Brother*, hit France in April and became an instant success, turning complete strangers into popular stars overnight. The year was also marked politically by the French presidential election campaign, which had direct repercussions on the media discourse surrounding *Amelie*, the film changing into an instrument of political discussion. Finally, the terrorist attack of September 11 caused such a shock all over the world that it may have indirectly influenced the international reception of *Amelie*, which was viewed as a feel-good antidote to the general malaise.[23] These aspects will be analysed in Chapter Four.

If 2001 was an exceptional year for French cinema, 2002 and 2003 marked a return to the harsh reality of globalised culture, and highlighted a number of important economic issues at stake. French popular cinema has increasingly become associated with intensive promotional strategies and consensual mainstream productions, and the results for these years showed a lower, yet stable market share of 35 per cent for French films. Although France fares better than other European countries, many articles voiced serious concern about the future of the French film industry, as the special issue of *Cinémaction* entitled 'What alternatives to Hollywood?' exemplified.[24] In order to place this situation into its context it is worth surveying briefly the evolution of French cinema in the last 20 years. I will focus on aspects that bear direct connections with Jeunet and *Amelie* in the areas of production, distribution, exhibition and reception.

Production and distribution contexts

In the 1980s and 1990s, the French film industry underwent changes which exacerbated the tension between cinema as a commercial venture and French film as an art form ('le septième art'). These have been discussed elsewhere,[25] and I will only briefly raise here a few issues that are relevant to the contextualisation of *Amelie*. Recently, film investments have increased, as have the number of films produced and their average budgets. Since 2000, about 180 French films have been produced annually, and the number of viewers has increased. In 2001 186 million tickets were sold, a 12 per cent increase on the previous year. This has coincided with significant structural changes, affecting the distribution and commercialisation of films in France. The emergence of multiplex screens and monthly passes, the development of home cinema and the multiplication of film channels on television have radically transformed film-watching habits, altering the balance between mainstream films and art cinema, the marketing of popular films and their distribution.

However, the situation of French cinema is not as clear-cut as it might seem. France dominates the European market, and substantial budgets are invested in the promotion of French films abroad, via the festival circuit and the work of Unifrance. The French film industry is often praised for its vitality and diversity, and retains a strong cultural image, but a number of structural changes have reshaped the notion of national identity. Recent trends include revisiting international co-productions, delocalising the shooting, and using English-language in French productions, which encourage the emergence of transnational actors/actresses. *Amelie*, for instance, is a Franco-German co-production, partly shot in Cologne for its indoor scenes.

As a result, the image of French cinema as an alternative to Hollywood is regularly questioned. Since the 1980s, the share of French films on the domestic market has been a growing cause for concern, with a turning point in 1986, when American films became more popular at the box office than French films. The market shares have since varied between 50 and 60 per cent in favour of American films, against about 30 per cent for French films, depending on the impact made by exceptional box office hits: for instance, Luc Besson's *Le Cinquième Elément/Fifth Element* salvaged the domestic statistics in 1997, bringing the French share up to 34.5 per cent, even if the film was arguably more an international venture than strictly French. Conversely, in the following year, *Titanic* (James Cameron, 1998) helped to sink the French share down to a 27.6 per cent low.

The 'unique' French system for funding the national film production has been extensively discussed and challenged in the last decade. Despite the lively production of first films, young film-makers find it increasingly difficult to finance their second or third films, and producers are more reluctant to take financial risks to support small, less commercial ventures. For instance, the merger of Vivendi with Universal in 2000 created the world's second largest media group, yet had a detrimental effect on the French production system. Vivendi's subsidiary, the pay channel Canal Plus, has been a major partner of French cinema since 1984, but it has reduced its contribution since 2001 as a result of the restructuring. The growing number of aborted projects and the increased concentration of the industry have also been identified as related issues that need to be addressed urgently.

Sometimes praised as the only way of preserving the French film industry and its diversity, the French system was also criticised as an unacceptable protectionist measure against the domination of American cinema. In 1993, the negotiations around the GATT agreements led to serious deliberations on film quotas and the circulation of cultural products.[26] In what is known as the 'cultural exception' debate, France (and Europe to an extent) took issue with the globalisation of culture, and demanded that cinema should be exempted from the liberal world-market agreements. Even within France, the support for 'cultural exception' was not unanimous. The CNC official report for 2001 highlighted concerns about 'real difficulties' and 'important changes' in the system, while recent analyses by Jean Cluzel and Fabrice Montebello even considered it a threat to the future of French cinema.[27]

The polarisation of auteur film and popular cinema

In November 2001, a special dossier devoted to the recent rejuvenation of French cinema appeared in the trade magazine *Le Film français*. It singled out technical innovations, creative and aesthetic trends, and the renewal of French heritage films that integrated more fantasy, action, and even violence, possibly in an attempt to embrace recent international trends in Hollywood and South Asian cinemas. One of their guest contributors was Jeunet, who placed the emphasis on 'quality':

> I think that there is a new generation of directors who are not afraid of trying to achieve the same quality as American films while retaining their cultural identity. [...] More generally, what links these films which have been successful at the box office is the quality that they strive for and openly put forward. None of them was produced with shoestring budgets, promoting the trendy sad and squalid atmosphere still advocated by some as a dogma. For those, success always looks suspect. The films which appeal to the critics and the public alike cause a panic in the post New-Wave's small circles.[28]

This sort of discourse takes us back to the production values and critical debate associated with the *Tradition de qualité*, denounced by the critics of *Cahiers du cinéma* in the 1950s, who then became the *auteurs*-directors of the French New Wave. Jeunet's position, following the steps of the likes of Luc Besson and Jean-Jacques Beineix, confirms that France is finally moving away from the powerful heritage of the New Wave. For example, a recent *Newsweek* article 'Crashing the New Wave' highlights the evolution towards more mainstream quality films, reporting that 'Gallic directors are back to making movies that people want to see, abroad as well as at home'.[29] It includes Luc Besson, Olivier Assayas, Mathieu Kassovitz and Jean-Pierre Jeunet in the new generation of French directors who 'still make "personal" films, but understand that their movies have to do well at the box office', and concludes that the 'distinct division between artistic and commercial that the New Wave created is coming to an end'.[30]

However, this type of Anglo-Saxon reading of the situation tends to be contradicted by the positions adopted by the French critical establishment and the polarisation between the films praised by the critics and those appealing to wider audiences has never been so visible in France. This translates into two distinct strands: on the one hand, as Fabrice Montebello argues, '*auteur* cinema [is] institutionalised as the norm of quality for French cinema',[31] by promoting authenticity and personal artistic projects expressing a personal vision of the world. On the other hand, commercial ventures that are more formatted in terms of their themes, casting and narrative pace are often critically ignored or dismissed as lacking in artistic merit. For example, the academic surveys on the young French cinema of the 1990s carried out by Michel Marie in 1998 and René Prédal in 2002, which discussed the renewal of French cinema, adopt an *auteurist* approach.[32] They both focus on the ongoing flow of new directors (including many women), highlighting in particular the diversity of first films and the new links between producers and film-makers.

Prédal has counted 450 newcomers between 1990 and 2000 for 150 films made every year.[33] According to him, however, France no longer has a quality mainstream cinema, and he certainly concentrates his own analysis on a young '*auteur* cinema', which does not attract wide audiences, choosing to ignore popular successes that in his view are not cinematographic (for example, Luc Besson's films or productions).[34] Prédal argues that this 'young French Cinema' is turned more towards realism and introspection than the visual, and it does not rely on technological prowess or special effects, but rather on elaborate *mise-en-scène*. In short, 'young French Cinema' is defined by what it is not, namely a spectacular, genre-based, big-budget cinema.[35]

Prédal's *auteur*-based approach to 'young French cinema' minimises the emergence, from the end of the 1990s, of a series of mainstream successes like the *Taxi* trilogy or *Yamakasi* (Ariel Zeitoun, 2001), produced by Luc Besson, and of films featuring comedians-turned-actors coming from television, such as Eric and Ramzy in *La Tour Montparnasse infernale* (Charles Nemes, 2001), all seen as popular entertainment alternatives to 'real cinema'. In this respect, Prédal's analysis meets the dominant perception of the French critical establishment.

Another example is Claude-Marie Trémois, who refers to the young French directors as 'the children of freedom', considering them the future of French cinema.[36] Trémois contrasts these 'young directors' explicitly with Jeunet and Caro, in a section entitled 'young film-makers already getting old', accusing them for taking themselves too seriously and producing alienating and disturbing films. It is easy to see why Jeunet and Caro's fantasy worlds should clash with the gritty social realism of the films of the 'young directors', but this differentiation, while illustrating the polarisation of French cinema, fails to highlight its diversity.

Despite their restricted audiences, the 'young directors' tended to be supported by the critical establishment, winning prizes, yet provoking a debate in the general press in reaction against their harsh treatment of social realist themes and crude naturalist filming style.[37] These films marked the 1990s and signalled a period of social malaise, but with a few exceptions, such as *Y aura-t-il de la neige à Noël/Will it Snow for Christmas* (Sandrine Veysset, 1997) and *La Vie rêvée des anges/Dream Life of Angels* (Zonca, 1998), they failed to attract wide audiences.

Although they are important to the identity of French cinema in other ways, small '*auteur*' films are sometimes criticised for benefiting from public funding without meeting their public in cinemas.[38] Because the critical attention that they receive often contrasts with their restricted audiences on the domestic market, there is a danger of portraying the marginal as the norm, thereby misrepresenting the French film industry as a whole. This is especially relevant when these films receive an international distribution, either in cinemas or on television, as a number of articles published in the British and American press in 2001–2002 illustrate.[39] Despite the fact that they present a distinctive vision of the world, Jeunet's films have tended to be associated more with popular cinema and glossy aesthetics, especially in French critical circles.

Look, ads and video clips: the postmodern aesthetics of the 1980s–1990s

If *auteur* cinema represents an important pole of French cinema's identity, at the other end of the scale, certain popular trends relevant to *Amelie* have been identified from the 1980s, evincing significant changes. By the end of the 1980s, a number of film-makers coming from television and/or publicity backgrounds, including Patrice Leconte, Etienne Chatiliez, Jean-Jacques Beineix and Luc Besson, had released films that revitalised French popular cinema with their own distinctive styles.[40]

Besson and Beineix in particular proposed a high-tech popular cinema, influenced by Hollywood, and appealing to young audiences, which became known as the *cinéma du look*.[41] Their early films promoted a glossy visual spectacle and 'advertising aesthetic', to quote Marie-Thérèse Journot's analysis of the crisis of modernity in the French cinema of the 1980s.[42] Although they soon reached international recognition, they had to withstand hostility from the critical establishment ranging from virulent attacks to indifference. However, they are now recognised internationally for contributing to the renewal of French popular cinema with varying degrees of success.[43]

Jeunet and Caro have been associated with *cinéma du look* on several accounts. Both *Delicatessen* and *La Cité des enfants perdus* were influenced stylistically by commercials and *bande dessinée* aesthetics, and the 'look' style. They contributed to the development of high-tech production values in the 1990s. They pioneered new digital film technologies, and helped the recognition of special effects company Duboi, which became established as a trademark of quality, recognised internationally. The emergence of new digital technologies within French cinema marked a renewal of the national film industry, seen by some – including Jeunet – as a new challenge, and by others as reviving the threats associated with the globalisation of cinema.[44]

With films like Beineix's *Diva* (1980) and *37°2 le matin/Betty Blue* (1986), or Besson's *Le Grand Bleu/The Big Blue* (1988), *cinéma du look* can also be read as the French illustration of the postmodern influence exerted on cinema from the 1980s onwards. This influence continued to prevail in the 1990s, underpinning, among others, the (rare) critical discussions of Jeunet and Caro's films, which represented postmodern fantasy worlds, shot in studio, and promoted visual effects rather than a realistic representation of the world. The postmodern framework often applied to *cinéma du look* will be used to map the analysis of *Amelie* in Chapters Two and Three.

So, despite the emphasis placed by the media on their distinctive style, it looks as though Jeunet and Caro were not so displaced after all from the French cinema landscape developing in the 1990s. They pioneered a number of trends that were subsequently copied and adopted in more popular forms, as the enthusiasm for spectacular visual effects in recent popular French cinema illustrates. After *La Cité des enfants perdus*, they parted amicably, mainly because they had different artistic ambitions: Caro moved towards experimental video and graphics, although he continued to work as an artistic designer – he contributed to *Vidocq* and *Blueberry*. He made a short film in 1998, *Exercice de Steel*, and a techno CD in 2000, and currently plans a first feature film.[45] Jeunet, on the other hand, was attracted to a less dark cinematic world, and wanted to make films with more artistic freedom and personal input. *Amelie* answered his interest in new technologies, while adopting an accessible narrative and drawing its style from the popular culture heritage. Its fantasy also confirmed that he had more in common with Méliès's tradition than with the more documentary approach of the Lumière brothers.

From notebook to storyboard: the genesis of the film

Amelie marks a turning point in Jeunet's career, but it also shows a coherent development of his previous work. Having collected ideas and anecdotes for a number of years, it was in 1998 that Jeunet apparently thought of constructing the narrative of his new film around the theme of solidarity, echoing the generalised national euphoria following the French victory in the football World Cup. For his first French solo project, Jeunet wanted to make a light personal film, moving away from Caro's darker influence and his more experimental approach to cinema:

> After *Alien*, I realised I had never made a truly positive film. This was of interest to me: building, rather than destroying presented me with a new, interesting challenge. I wanted to make a sweet film at this point in my career and life, to see if I could make people dream and give them pleasure. This is my personal film, one I had dreamed about for a long time.[46]

Amelie is thus a personal project realised, to a certain extent, in the spirit of the French *auteurist* tradition of filming what one knows well. Jeunet claimed that he carried the film inside him for 25 years, collecting personal memories, such as the idea of the marbles in the schoolyard, or that of the suicidal goldfish, before inserting them into the screenplay.[47] One of his objectives was to re-create the atmosphere of his childhood: 'I was born in 1953 and I have retained some nostalgia for the France of my childhood, or rather for its images, its fashion, and its objects.'[48] This took different forms in the film, from references to brand names and old toys, to old-fashioned indoor sets like the caretaker's lodge.

Another determining factor in the film's genesis was the meeting with writer, press photographer and collector Michel Folco, who had shown Jeunet an unusual album consisting of a collection of anonymous passport photographs that inspired one of the storylines of the film.[49] Jeunet had also seen *Les Ruses du diable* (Paul Vecchiali, 1954), in which a young woman sees her life transformed when she starts finding a FF 100 note in the street every day. After considering a number of options for the title, including 'Amélie des Abbesses', it was a Sacha Guitry film, *Le Destin fabuleux de Désirée Clary* (1942), that inspired the original French title of the film (the international distributors adopted shorter titles, *Amelie from Montmartre* in America and *Amelie* in Britain).

It took over a year and 18 drafts to complete the screenplay for *Amelie*. Jeunet called in Guillaume Laurant, who had already worked with him on *La Cité des enfants perdus*. The former focused on the segmentation of the film and storyboard, while the latter, also a playwright and novelist, was responsible for the dialogue. Laurant was credited with a number of original ideas, such as that of the street prompter hidden in a cellar providing Amélie with witty cues.

The film was prepared using a storyboard, composed of cartoon-like sketches illustrating key visual scenes of the film at pre-production stage. Until recently, storyboards were little used in France,[50] although they had been recognised as effective tools by such prestigious film-makers as Georges Méliès, Fritz Lang and Alfred Hitchcock. Beyond serving the purpose of reassuring producers with concrete information, they can also inform decisions involving large budgets or original fantasy worlds. Drawing on the forms and codes of comic strip, the storyboard provides valuable information on the genesis of the film, as well as on the director's working method, since it visualises the imagery and explicates the creative project of the film. It is hardly surprising that Jeunet, whose cinema is overtly influenced by animation and *bande dessinée*, should view the storyboard as an attractive, time-saving working tool, the first material rendering of a visual mental image:

> I do storyboards – not for actors, but for the visual scene. I hate to waste time on the set. On the set, you have to keep a good pace, because the clock is your master. For that reason, I have to know exactly what I'm trying to do beforehand. I spend about two months doing the storyboards. I'm very slow, and I do everything myself. I remember spending three days changing the size of something I had sketched because I felt it was too small. Before the storyboards, I wrote 18 drafts of the script.[51]

The storyboard of *Amelie* was published in 2001 in the first issue of *Synopsis*, then in a more comprehensive book form in 2004, including original drawings by Luc Desportes and interviews. It contains sketches drawn in the first instance by Jeunet, who then asked Desportes to provide more precise drawings: 'Desportes knows me well enough to draw what I want, but that I cannot draw myself. [...] My sketch and a short explanatory note are enough for him to know what to do.'[52]

The storyboard is a useful way of communicating information to the crew, especially for the frame, the lighting, the positioning of the camera, the set and the costume designs. For the cinephile spectator or the critic performing a textual analysis, it becomes a valuable tool of comparison with the finished product, reinforcing the impression that the film was visualised in Jeunet's mind before the shooting. For example, a detailed study of the storyboard suggests that Jeunet had a mental vision of the scenes (*le découpage*) and specific frames at an early stage of the creation process. The sketches also indicate that Jeunet had a clear image of his heroine in mind before casting Audrey Tautou for the part.

Reforming the troupe: the production team and the crew

A French and German co-production

Retrospectively, it is evident that the huge success of *Amelie* partly masked Jeunet's initial difficulties in launching the production of the film. As Jean-Pierre Lavoignat's documentary film shows,[53] he had to overcome many obstacles, including the withdrawal of his intended main star, cinematographer and music composer. His most serious challenge, however, was to find a financial package, despite his reputation, his Hollywood experience and the cult status of the previous two films. After French major Pathé expressed interest and pulled out, competitor UGC (Brigitte Maccioni), which had already played a part in the financing of Jeunet and Caro's previous films, took on the production of the film. In addition, Claudie Ossard, who had produced *Delicatessen* and *La Cité des enfants perdus*, as well as other important French ventures of the 1980s, such as *37°2 le matin*, was hired by UGC, bringing into the project her own company, Victoires Productions.

The financial package was as follows: UGC brought in FF 27 m and was in charge of the distribution of the film and the international rights; the pay channel Canal Plus FF 19 m; F3 (French national TV channel) FF 8 m; Sofica Sofinergie (television and film financing company) FF 4 m; Victoires Productions for FF 1.9 m. The German co-producers contributed FF 16m, which corresponds to 22 per cent of the total budget. A bid was made for two grants: the *Avances sur recettes*, a French selective subsidy scheme for French film projects based on the redistribution of taxes levied from the cinema tickets, TV channels and video incomes, and the European production aid fund *Eurimages*. Both bids were unsuccessful.[54]

The official budget of the film is recorded at FF 76.58 m, which corresponds roughly to $12 m. Within the French context, *Amelie* can thus be considered a relatively large-budget film, as the average production cost for 2001 was estimated by the CNC to be FF 26 m ($4 m). However, several 2001 films had much larger budgets: Pitof's digital film *Vidocq* is estimated to have cost over FF 150 m, while *Le Pacte des loups* reached FF 200 m. By Hollywood standards, of course, *Amelie* had a modest budget: *Alien: Resurrection*, for example cost $70 m in 1997 (see Table 2 in Appendix 2).

The budget of *Amélie* was allocated as follows: FF 7 m (about ten per cent of the overall budget) went to the actors' wages, which was modest for a film with a large cast, even if none of them were bankable stars at the time of the casting. A comparable budget was devoted to the costumes and sets, while the postproduction cost FF 16 m. Around FF 11 m (15 per cent of the total budget) was used to finance its innovative marketing campaign, discussed in Chapter Four.

Shooting Amelie

After three months of preparation, the shooting of *Amelie*, shared between France and Germany, lasted 20 weeks (from 2 March to 7 July 2000). Most of *Amelie*'s indoor sets were built in Cologne. But the decision to shoot the film partly on location in the centre of Paris proved the most difficult challenge for Jeunet, who had so far mainly worked in studio, and was reputed for his perfectionist taste for impeccable image composition.

In his 'Leçon de cinéma', an interview with Laurent Tirard, Jeunet provides useful pointers about his working methods. He always uses a camcorder to prepare the shots, and prints still photographs for the crew. He is especially careful to aim for fluidity when planning camera movements. Tracking shots have to be regular to look elegant, which is not always possible, according to him, when using a steadycam.[55] Thanks to digital timing technology, Jeunet can view his work without having to wait for the rushes, and activate the digital transfer process, which directly affects the shooting. As a result, colour manipulation, for example, adds an extra stage to the traditional work of *mise-en-scène*.

Although 2001 saw the explosion of digital technology in French cinema, it remained a costly tool mainly reserved for a minority of French films. At the time, some critics found fault with Jeunet, as they had done in the 1980s with the *cinéma du look*, for his overusing technology for its own sake, and for creating expensive empty visual effects (see Chapter Four). More significantly, digital film-making redefined and extended the roles of the technical crew.

Amelie's technical crew

The majority of *Amelie*'s technical crew had worked with Jeunet previously: Aline Bonetto for the art direction and set designs, Madeline Fontaine for the costumes, Hervé Schneid in charge of the editing and Gérard Hardy for the sound. The most significant newcomer was the director of cinematography, Bruno Delbonnel, a personal friend and former collaborator of Jeunet's who was given the difficult task of replacing Darius Khondji, who was engaged on other projects. Khondji's camera skills had proved a major factor in the success of the previous films by introducing vibrant colours and effective indoor sets. Delbonnel's tasks included the lighting of sets as well as the selection of specific lenses for distinctive short focal length. He was allowed artistic freedom of action and the financial means to achieve complicated set-ups, including cranes and heavy lighting equipment for night shots.[56] Duboi and

Les Versaillais were once again in charge of the special effects and completed the technical team (see Chapter Three).

Extending the nuclear family: the cast of *Amelie*

The actors of *Delicatessen* and *La Cité des enfants perdus* had been noted for their distinctive features. Once again, for *Amelie*, Jeunet took an active part in the casting of the actors, starting with Audrey Tautou.

Audrey Tautou (Amélie Poulain)

It is difficult today to imagine Amélie played by any actress other than Audrey Tautou, who stands out as the 'revelation' of 2001, and France's new star. The success of the film clearly rests upon her charm, physical appearance and performance, and this role has had a tremendous impact on her budding career.

Born in 1978, Tautou grew up in Auvergne in a middle-class family. As a child she wanted to be a primate specialist. At 18, she came to Paris to study literature and also enrolled in an established private drama school, le Cours Florent. Before she was chosen for the role of Amélie, she had appeared in supporting parts in several films, including Tonie Marshall's comedy *Vénus Beauté (Institut)* (1999), for which she received the César for Most Promising Young Actress in 2000.

Jeunet first saw Tautou's face on the poster for this film, and called her in for a casting audition, after Emily Watson, who had been approached for the

Figure 1: Audrey Tautou as Amélie.

part, declined it for personal reasons. According to Jeunet, Tautou was chosen immediately: 'She has the innocence and the determination that I needed for her character. She is an elf... she also is everything that I like in an actress: precise, rigorous and full of fantasy.'[57] It is difficult to assess to what extent Jeunet launched Tautou's career. Their partnership had extraordinary consequences for both, to such an extent that she was from its conception at the centre of his next project, *Un long dimanche de fiançailles*.

Thanks to *Amelie*, Tautou's gamine face has become world-famous, turning her instantly into a star, an icon and a symbol of Frenchness. As Ginette Vincendeau points out, Tautou is emblematic in the sense that she 'crystallises and authenticates' the social values of her time.[58] She has acquired a modern child-woman persona and developed a performance style based on naturalness and ingenuity, which will be discussed in Chapter Two. Often seen as 'an ideal daughter' type and an unthreatening form of young femininity, her fan base is wide and includes young audiences who feel they can relate to her.

The role of Amélie, with which Tautou remains associated in the eye of the public and the media, transformed her career. Her other films made immediately before *Amelie*, *Le Battement d'ailes du papillon/Happenstance* (Laurent Firode, 2000), or, just after, *A la Folie, pas du tout/He Loves me, He Loves me not* (Pascale Bailly, 2001), received an international distribution against all odds, mainly because she featured in them. She was offered starring roles in films of international stature such as *Dirty Pretty Things* (Stephen Frears, 2002) and *Nowhere To Go But Up* (Amos Gitai, 2003). With *Un long dimanche de fiançailles*, she became the best-paid French actress for 2003.[59] Her international stature has since been extended further with her selection over a number of established French stars for co-starring with Tom Hanks in the adaptation of Dan Brown's bestseller, Ron Howard's *The Da Vinci Code*, released in 2006.

Mathieu Kassovitz (Nino Quincampoix)

By the time Mathieu Kassovitz (born 1967) appeared in *Amelie*, he was already an established French director thanks to the success of *La Haine/Hate* (1995) and *Les Rivières pourpres/Crimson Rivers* (2000). However, he had been equally acknowledged as an actor, with major parts in Jacques Audiard's *Regarde les hommes tomber/See How They Fall* (1994) and *Un Héros très discret/Self-Made Hero* (1996).

Kassovitz has the looks of a young leading man and the personality of a rebel. No director so far had cast him as a romantic hero, despite his looks. Since *Amelie*, however, he has increased his international fame and become one of the faces of Lancôme in a high-profile publicity campaign for their perfume 'Miracle', designed for 'a man who brings his dreams to life – a man who takes hold of his destiny and makes it happen'. He is seen by the cosmetic firm as

Figure 2: Nino (Mathieu Kassovitz).

embodying the contemporary, artistic, bold man, and is described thus on their website: 'Mathieu's determination and spice for life shine through, not only in his work but also in his persona. A sophisticated, urban and charismatic man, he is a figure that represents empowerment coupled with the elegance and style of Lancôme.'[60] In 2001, Kassovitz was listed in the *Newsweek* poll of the most influential men, and he played alongside Nicole Kidman in a British comedy *Birthday Girl* (Tom Butterworth, 2001). Like Jeunet, Kassovitz has worked in America as a director since *Amelie*, accepting a high-profile commission to direct *Gothika* (2003), starring Halle Berry, which opened doors into Hollywood, even if the film had a mixed reception.

Jeunet's extended 'family'

The film displays a gallery of secondary characters around Amélie, recalling the colourful supporting roles of the classical age of French cinema. These characters are 'ordinary people' representative of the popular classes, yet their faces somehow are memorable. They re-invent a microcosm of society, with a series of easily identified cartoon-like social types: the concierge, the tobacconist, the grocer, the painter, the barmaid and the writer.

Casting was a crucial stage of the pre-production process. Jeunet favoured actors with stage experience, forming a sort of extended family, with regulars like Dominique Pinon, Rufus and Serge Merlin. In *Amelie*, most of the newcomers were known for their stage careers, but others like Jamel Debbouze and Yolande Moreau came from stand-up comedy and television. This diversity of experience coloured the actors' performances, while illustrating the mobility of French artists across different media.

Dominique Pinon (born 1955) plays Joseph, the manic jealous lover who sits in *Les Deux Moulins* all day sniggering and recording on tape a sort of diary of the smallest activities of his ex-lover, the waitress Gina. Alternating between film and stage performances, Pinon is known as Jeunet's fetish actor, and has featured in all his films. Not initially cast in *Amelie*, he insisted on taking part in the film, adding substance to an initially minor supporting role. Pinon's unusual looks are often connected to cartoon characters; he is known for extraordinary graphic distortions of his face, used to spectacular effect in *Delicatessen* and *La Cité des enfants perdus*. In *Amelie*, it serves a humorous purpose, and enhances the grumpy disposition of the character.

Rufus (born 1942) is another member of Jeunet's cinematic family with parts in *Delicatessen* and *La Cité des enfants perdus*. A distinguished stage and film actor since the 1960s, he belongs to a tradition of left-wing political theatre – he started at the Café de la Gare in the early 1980s, before performing in many plays and writing some himself. Also known for his supporting roles in French cinema, he has worked with such prestigious directors as Jean-Luc Godard, Claude Lelouch and Georges Lautner. He plays Amélie's father, a retired doctor and a widower who lives alone in Enghien, a Paris suburb, and cannot express affection for his daughter. As is often the case, Rufus constructs the character of an idiosyncratic dreamer, helped by his lanky physical appearance and bony features. There is an element of the absurd in his character.

Serge Merlin plays Amélie's neighbour, Raymond Dufayel, a recluse painter who has a rare disease that makes his bones so brittle and fragile that he has to avoid any physical contact, hence his nickname 'the man of glass'. He had a part in *La Cité des enfants perdus*, but most of his career has been on the stage. Taking on a role that had initially been offered to Jean-Louis Trintignant and Michel Serrault, Merlin brought some personal touches to his character, including wearing his own hat in the film.

Born in 1975 in a Moroccan family, Jamel Debbouze was brought up in France and he belongs to the growing band of 'beur' comedians and actors, who are the children of North-African immigrants born and brought up in France. Before his role in *Amelie*, Debbouze was well known in France as a cult stand-up and television comedian specialising in comic sketches about life in the French banlieues and 'beur' identity. He also appeared in two films, *Le Ciel, les oiseaux... et ta mère* (Jamel Bensalah, 1998) and *Zonzon* (Laurent Bouhnik, 1998). It is on the strength of the latter that Jeunet selected him for the part of the simple-minded and sensitive greengrocer assistant Lucien. Debbouze plays the only 'non-white' character in the cast, and his character became the object of much discussion after the film's release, as will be explained in Chapter Four. For this role, full use is made of his vulnerable physical appearance and disability (he lost an arm in a train accident at 13). Unlike in his shows, where he is never still and displays tremendous physical energy, his performance style in *Amelie* is subdued, and it is more through his stutter and broken speech that Lucien evokes Jamel the comedian. Following the huge success of *Astérix and Obélix: Mission Cléopâtre* in 2002, in which he stole the show from established stars like Gérard Depardieu and Christian Clavier, Debbouze has become a bankable popular star of the French younger generation.

Other supporting roles include Isabelle Nanty as Georgette, the café tobacconist who develops the symptoms of a new obscure illness every day. Nanty is known in France as a comic in films and on stage, but also as a stage director. She directed her first film, *Le Bison*, in 2003. In *Amelie*, she affects a drawling Eastern accent, which evokes Jeunet's origins, while delivering memorable dialogue. Claire Maurier is Suzanne, the owner of *Les Deux Moulins*, and a former circus artist who was the victim of a passionate love affair, illustrating Jeunet's taste for bizarre secondary characters. Her main claim to fame in the cinema is that she played Antoine Doinel's mother in *Les 400 Coups* (François Truffaut, 1959), a connection that Jeunet explores in several ways: Amélie and Antoine share common traits, as neglected children who take refuge in their imaginary worlds, and two other direct references are made to Truffaut's cinema in *Amelie* a short clip from *Jules et Jim* and the flight of the pigeons recalling a scene from *Les 400 Coups*. However, Maurier (born 1929) is mainly a stage actress, although she recently appeared as the mother in *Un air de famille* (Cédric Klapisch, 1996).

A newcomer to Jeunet's world, Yolande Moreau was brought to public notice in the 1990s by the daily surreal comic sketches on Canal Plus, as part of the satirical group *Les Deschiens*. She has played supporting roles in a number of films, including *Sans toit ni loi* (Agnès Varda, 1985), and made her directorial debut in 2004 with *Quand la mer monte*, in which she also starred. In *Amelie*, Moreau plays a lonely concierge whose performance is based upon a general languid demeanour yet mobile facial expression.

Urbain Cancelier has had supporting parts in various French films from the 1980s (*Le Bossu*, Philippe de Broca, 1997) before playing Collignon, the grocer. In addition to many supporting roles in films, Maurice Bénichou is mainly known for stage performances, having worked, for example, with the English director Peter Brooks. He plays Bretodeau, the sensitive middle-aged man who becomes the first beneficiary of Amelie's altruistic project. Artus de Penguern has worked as a cinema actor since the 1980s with Maurice Pialat and in mainstream comedies. He has made short films and wrote a one-man show in the 1990s, before making his directorial debut in 2001 with *Grégoire Moulin contre l'humanité*. He plays one of the café's customers, Hipolito the failed writer. Claude Perron has an acting career that is mostly associated with Albert Dupontel's films. She plays Eva, the sex-shop assistant, and Nino's colleague. Clotilde Mollet is an actress and musician. She has appeared in supporting roles in films and on stage from the 1990s. She plays Gina, a waitress at *Les Deux Moulins*.

Although these parts are secondary, some of them little more than cameos, they all contribute to the quaint originality often associated with the film. Jeunet attaches a great deal of importance to actor direction and likes to adapt his strategy to the actor's personality. For example, in *Amelie*, Audrey Tautou tended to follow the script closely, while Jamel Debbouze, Isabelle Nanty and Yolande Moreau were more inclined to improvise. One of Jeunet's favourite 'tricks' during shooting was to surprise the actors by making last minute changes in the script or a detail of *mise-en-scène* to initiate spontaneous reactions.

The study of the production contexts of *Amelie* has unveiled a number of contradictions. On the one hand, what was initially a small personal film and a turning point in Jeunet's career has turned into an uncontrollable, social, cultural and media phenomenon. On the other hand, its exceptional success cannot be reduced to its being released at the right time and capturing an ethereal 'air du temps'. *Amelie* undoubtedly created a surprise, as Jeunet was the first to admit. However, this chapter has shown that the film was also the outcome of a long-term, clearly thought-out project and careful pre-production work, as well as the meeting of a director and an actress. It is now time to turn to the film itself and focus on a more textual analysis.

Notes

1   R. Pride, 'Magnificent obsession', *Filmmaker* (Autumn 2001) pp.52–55.
2   P. Eisenreich, '*Un long dimanche de fiançailles*: la marque du vampire', *Positif* 525 (November 2004), p.6.
3   Caro was a contributor for *Métal hurlant*, *Fluide glacial*, *L'Echo des savanes*. Caro and Jeunet co-wrote essays on Tex Avery, Jacques Rouxel (Shadoks) and the Fleischer brothers (Betty Boop and Popeye).
4   *Bande dessinée* is France's 'ninth art' and an important cultural phenomenon (28 m books sold in 2000). See A. Miller, 'Bande dessinée', in H. Dauncey (ed.), *French Popular Culture: An Introduction* (London: Arnold, 2003), pp.135–149.
5   Examples include *Astérix et Obélix contre César* (Claude Zidi, 1999); *Astérix et Obélix: Mission Cléopâtre* (Alain Chabat, 2002); *Blueberry* (Jan Kounen, 2004); *L'Enquête corse* (Alain Berbérian, 2004); or *Les Dalton* (Philippe Haïm, 2004).
6   See, for example, the commercial films for Lactel, Buggy or Malabar. The musical video-clips include 'La Fille aux bas nylon' in 1984 and 'Hélène' in 1987 for Julien Clerc, 'Zoolook' in 1984 for Jean-Michel Jarre, 'Tombé pour la France' in 1986 for Etienne Daho. For more information, see Jeunet's official website, http://jpjeunetlesite.online.fr, accessed on 14 December 2004.
7   For instance, Jeunet wrote a humorous summary of *Alien* in the September 1980 issue of *Fluide glacial*.
8   J.-J. Bernard, 'Charcuterie fine', *Première* 170 (May 1991), pp.78–83 (p.80). The film did not obtain subsidies nor television co-production advances.
9   The film's production information comes from Jeunet's commentary on the DVD.
10   This concise account of the film and its reception is based on several French reviews which voice similar opinions on the film and its influences: J.-M. Frodon, '*La Cité des enfants perdus* ou le carnaval des hybrides', *Le Monde*, 19 May 1995; G. Lefort and O. Séguret, 'Une cité interdite', *Libération*, 18 May 1995; A. Coppermann, 'Somptueuse et froide fantasmagorie', *Les Echos*, 18 May 1995 and S. Kaganski, 'Le septième artifice', *Les Inrockuptibles*, 7 May 1995.

11 J. Michaud and C. D'Yvoire, 'La Cité des enfants perdus', Studio Magazine 99 (May 1995), p.71. This is more than in Steven Spielberg's Jurassic Park (1994).

12 See short note in Première 224 (November 1995), p.58.

13 J.-Y. Katelan, 'La Cité des enfants perdus', and A. Kruger, 'Caro et Jeunet: les faux jumeaux', Première 219 (June 1995), pp.43 and 115–120; J. Michaud and C. D'Yvoire, Studio Magazine 98 (May 1995), pp.10, 66–73. In the daily press, see reviews by Frodon, Coppermann, Lefort and Kaganski cited in note 10.

14 He had also been approached for The Addams Family 2 (Kruger: 1995, p.118).

15 See R. Ebert, Chicago Sun-Times, 1997, and the press review of the film in E. Ezra, 'Resurrecting the Alien director: Jean-Pierre Jeunet in Hollywood', New Cinemas 1: 1 (2002), pp.54–60 (p.55).

16 Quoted in D. Thomson, The Alien Quartet (London: Bloomsbury, 1998), p.137. See also Jeunet's interviews: Bayon, 'Se forger des nerfs en acier trempé', Libération, 12 November 1997, p.29; J.-A. Bondy, Alien 4, Première 246 (September 1997), pp.86–90; J.-Y. Katelan and E. Libiot, 'Elixir de Jeunet', Première 249 (December 1997), pp.86–91; L. Tirard, 'La leçon de cinéma de Jean-Pierre Jeunet', Studio Magazine, Hors Série 1997, pp.122–127.

17 Statistics are from Thomson 1998, p.180, and the IMDb website. In France, the film was released in November 1997 (450 prints), attracting 2.6 m viewers. It was Première's 'film of the month' in December 1997 (p.35).

18 The screenplay was by Josh Whedon, who also wrote Toy Story (John Lasseter, 1995).

19 This was not matched in subsequent years until the success of Christophe Barratier's Les Choristes/The Chorus in 2004.

20 S. Jeffries, 'Depardieu steals the digital thunder', The Observer, 26 August 2001. George Lucas had hoped to premiere this technology with Star Wars: Episode 2.

21 F. Meaux Saint-Marc, 'A taste for the spectacular', Screen International, 12 January 2001, p.60.

22 O. Séguret, 'Le Démarrage de 2001 est exceptionnel', Libération, 26 February 2001.

23 See the explicit titles of Anglo-American reviews, such as D. Howe, 'Amélie shines in the City of Light', Washington Post, 9 November 2001, or B. Ellen, 'A spoonful of sugar…', Times, 4 October 2001, pp.11–13.

24 'Quelle diversité face à Hollywood?', Cinémaction, Hors Série 2002, contains an essay by P. d'Hughes, 'Une Amélie ne fait pas le printemps' (pp.182–187), identifying serious problems in the French film industry, which should not disappear behind the successes of 2001. They are confirmed by other alarmist articles, such as C. Pardo, 'Un art noyé dans la marchandise: mort programmée du cinéma français', Le Monde diplomatique, July 2001, p.25, and 'Entre succès fragiles et loi de l'argent: le cinéma indépendant marginalisé', Monde diplomatique, May 2003, p.27; P. Mérigeau, 'Chant du coq, chant du cygne: le cinéma français va-t-il si bien?', Nouvel Observateur 1939 (3 January 2002); and more balanced editorials by David Kessler in the CNC's Bilan 2002 287 (May 2003), p.3, and Bilan 2003 290 (May 2004), p.3.

25 For a more detailed account of the French film industry, see L. Creton and A. Jäckel 'Business 1960–2004: a certain idea of the film industry', in M. Temple and M. Witt (eds), The French Cinema Book (London: BFI, 2004), especially pp.215–220.

26 A discussion of these issues is beyond the scope of this book, but, for more information, see for example, Temple and Witt: 2004, p.190, or S. Regourd, L'Exception culturelle (Paris: Presses Universitaires de France, 2002).

27 Kessler: 2002, p.3. See also F. Montebello, Le Cinéma en France (Paris: Armand Colin, 2005), pp.177–204, and J. Cluzel, Propos impertinents sur le cinéma français (Paris: Presses Universitaires de France, 2003), pp.48–49.

28 Jeunet, in S. Dacbert, 'Trois réalisateurs adeptes de la simplicité…et du public', Le Film français 2911 (23 November 2001), p.19.

29 D. Thomas, 'Crashing the New Wave', Newsweek, 20 May 2002, p.66.

30 Thomas: 2002, p.66.

31 Montebello: 2005, p.192.

28   AMELIE

32   M. Marie (ed.), *Le Jeune cinéma français* (Paris: Nathan, 1998); R. Prédal, *Le Jeune cinéma français* (Paris: Nathan, 2002).

33   Prédal: 2002, p.2.

34   Prédal: 2002, p.4.

35   Prédal: 2002, p.95. Also used by Chris Darke in a feature article in *Sight and Sound*, the phrase takes on a different meaning, emphasising the contradictions of the new directors of the 1990s ('The Group: Young French Cinema', December 1999, pp.24–27).

36   C.-M. Trémois, *Les Enfants de la liberté* (Paris: Seuil, 1997), pp.245–248. The 'young directors' discussed by Trémois include Erick Zonca, Bruno Dumont, Xavier Beauvois, Arnaud Desplechin, Cédric Klapisch, Marion Vernoux and Laetitia Masson.

37   For example, see C. Pardo, 'Crime, Pornographie et mépris: des films français fascinés par le sordide', *Monde diplomatique*, February 2000, p.28, who deplores the sordid and abject turn in French cinema, which 'revelled in despair, decadence, dead ends, powerlessness and murder', quoted in M. Scatton-Tessier, 'Le Petisme: flirting with the sordid in *Le Fabuleux destin d'Amélie Poulain*', 2004, p.198.

38   Cluzel: 2003, pp.10–11.

39   See, for example, S.F. Said, 'French Resistance', *Daily Telegraph*, 24 March 2001, and Thomas: 2002, p.66.

40   For example *Les Spécialistes/The Specialists* (Patrice Leconte, 1986, 5.3 m in France), *La Vie est un long fleuve tranquille/Life is a Long Quiet River* (Etienne Chatiliez, 1987, 3 m), *Le Grand Bleu* (9m) and *37.2° le matin* (3.6 m).

41   See S. Harris, 'The cinéma du look', in E. Ezra (ed.), *European Cinema* (Oxford: Oxford University Press, 2003), pp.219–232.

42   M.-T. Journot, '*L'Esthétique publicitaire' dans le cinéma français des années 80: la modernité en crise* (Paris: L'Harmattan, 2004).

43   See S. Hayward, *Luc Besson* (Manchester: Manchester University Press, 1998), and P. Powrie, *Jean-Jacques Beineix* (Manchester: Manchester University Press, 2001). Besson is now an international director and producer. He writes screenplays and children's books. Beineix's rare recent films have been commercial flops (*Mortel transfert*, 2001) and he has turned to writing comic books.

44   See, for example, James Austin, who argues that the Americanisation of French cinema can also be read as a gallicised version of an American cinema often associated with special effects. J. Austin, 'Digitizing frenchness in 2001: on a historic moment in the French cinema', *French Cultural Studies*, 2004, pp.281–299.

45   *Dante 01*, a science fiction small-budget film, is to be released in 2007.

46   Jeunet in Pride: 2001, pp.52–55.

47   Jeunet repeatedly states in the DVD commentary that he can remember these scenes from his own childhood and that they are reproduced in the film as he remembers them.

48   Quoted in G. Vincendeau, 'Café society', *Sight and Sound* 11: 8 (August 2001), p.23.

49   B. Vallaeys, 'A l'origine, l'album maniaque de Michel Folco', *Libération*, 25 April 2001. S. Voiturin, 'Amélie Poulain fabuleusement sublime', *Sonovision* 451 (May 2001), pp.14–17.

50   In recent years in France, renewed interest for storyboarding has been confirmed by the growing number of exhibitions, together with publications and a new magazine *Storyboard*.

51   Jeunet in S.Tobias, 'Jean-Pierre Jeunet', *The Onion A.V. Club*, 31 October 2001. Website http://avclub.theonion.com/avclub3739/bonusfeature1_3739.html, accessed on 24 September 2003.

52   J.-P. Jeunet, G. Laurant and L. Desportes, in *Le Fabuleux destin d'Amélie Poulain*, Collection Storyboard, (Paris: Alvisa, 2004), p.6.

53   'Le Fabuleux destin d'Amélie Poulain', documentary made by Jean-Pierre Lavoignat for a special Jeunet evening on Canal Plus on 4 September 2004.

54   The finance plan was published in *Ecran Total* 382 (5 September 2001), p.16. Other statistics are provided by Claudie Ossard in P. Escande and M. Esquirou, 'Claudie Ossard: Les films que je fais sont ceux que j'aime', *Les Echos*, 17 May 2001.

55   In Tirard: 1997, p.125.

56   See interview in Y. Clanet and J.L. Deriaz, 'Amélie from Montmartre', *ARRI News* 9 (2001), Website, http://www.arri.com/infodown/news/0109_e.pdf, pp.8–11, accessed on 23 April 2004.

57   J.-P. Lavoignat, 'Le Paris de Jean-Pierre Jeunet', *Studio Magazine* 158 (July 2000), p.14.

58   See G. Vincendeau, 'Miss France', *Sight and Sound*, February 2005, pp.12–15 (p.14).

59   E. Berretta, 'Les Millions des stars', *Le Point*, 6 May 2004, p.86.

60   See Kassovitz's profile on the Lancôme website: http://www.lancome-usa.com/_us/_en/about/discoverlancome/lancomefaces/mathieu/mathieu_beauty.aspx, accessed on 2 February 2005.

2 Something old, something new: *Amelie*'s narrative

'She likes schemes... but what about her own life?' (Dufayel)

Bringing together a character-based narrative and a distinctive style, the film relies on the pace of the story-telling, as much as on its eccentric heroine, Amélie Poulain. This chapter examines the film's narrative structure, its use of time and space, generic hybridity and diverse influences. It also provides a detailed character study of Amélie, whose iconicity and charisma significantly contributed to the success of the film.

Narrative structure: Amélie's quest

Plot development

As suggested by its French title, *Amelie* focuses on the destiny of Amélie Poulain, around whom the whole film narrative is organised. A waitress in a Montmartre café, Amélie suddenly finds a meaning to her life by devoting her time and energy to improving the lot of the people around her. The structure of the film can be segmented into 12 main sections.

Table 1: Segmentation of *Amelie*

1. A 20-minute prologue, using voiceover narration, retraces Amélie's childhood, from her conception in 1973 to the time when the story really starts in 1997, and introduces the film's main characters.

2. Amélie discovers the treasure box in her flat on 30 August 1997, just as she hears of Princess Diana's death on television.

3. Amélie investigates to identify the owner of the box. She meets various neighbours in the process (the concierge, the painter, the grocer's parents...) and eventually tracks down Dominique Bretodeau. She first meets Nino on the metro platform: love at first sight.

4. Amélie returns the box anonymously, witnesses Bretodeau's reaction and decision to renew contact with his family. Amélie's new-found joy in helping others triggers her decision to help repair the lives of the people around her.

5. She immediately begins by helping the blind man in the street. She then stages her first scheme. She steals her father's garden gnome, and misses the last train.

6. Nino loses his photo album while chasing the bald man in the red shoes. From then on, Amélie tries to track him down. She confides in her neighbour the painter.

7. Amélie devises more schemes. She plays matchmaker between Georgette and Joseph at the café; she borrows the key and rigs the grocer's flat as a revenge for his cruelty to Lucien.

8. Looking for Nino: Amélie visits the sex shop where Nino works and talks to Eva. She plays hide-and-seek with him in Sacré-Coeur, the Foire du Trône, in the metro and the train stations.

9. Nino is now looking for Amélie too. Amélie reads the concierge's letters and creates a new fake one. The mystery of the bald man in the red shoes is ` solved. She sets a meeting with Nino at the café, but can't bring herself to introduce herself.

10. Amélie arranges another rendez-vous in the station, to reveal to Nino the identity of the bald man in the red shoes. She remains hidden. The supposedly lost letter arrives in the concierge's letter box.

11. Amélie bakes a cake dreaming about happiness. Nino knocks on the door. She hides. He goes away. She watches the painter's tape. He returns. She opens the door. They kiss.

12. Epilogue: the two lovers embark on their romance driving round Paris on a scooter. All the subplots are resolved.

Amelie combines conventional plot development and characterisation with heterogeneous narrative forms. The discovery of the box acts as the turning point of the main narrative, triggering the heroine's interest in other people, and her quest for her own destiny. The ending provides the clear and unambiguous closure of romantic comedy and fairytales. The story unfolds chronologically, even though it also incorporates an amalgam of interludes, digressions and subplots grafted onto the main narrative, including flashbacks, and childhood memories.

Blended into her routine, recurrent visits are made into Amélie's imaginary world and thoughts, often as a structuring device within the narrative. Her day-dreaming becomes embedded into reality, occasionally triggering a reaction. For instance, it is while imagining her own memorial tribute on television that she decides to reactivate her father's taste for travel. Similarly, fake subtitles are used in a Russian film extract to provide mediated access to her intimate thoughts, following a discussion with Dufayel. As for Nino's extravagant adventures in Afghanistan, they are imagined in a desperate attempt to explain his absence at their rendezvous and overcome her despair.

More generally, the plot unfolds in a series of episodes triggered by cause and effect relationships, chance and destiny. Secondary characters are introduced for self-standing digressions, yet they are connected by familiar motifs, namely the quest for personal identity and place within the local community. In addition, the film is informed by a series of *faits divers* (small news items) found in the press, which feed the narrative in different ways, the most notable being Princess Diana's car accident, which turned into a global news item.[1] A number of mysteries need to be solved: who is the owner of the treasure box? What is the mysterious young woman in the Renoir painting thinking about?[2] Who is the bald man who features in the discarded photographs in Nino's album? How does the garden gnome travel the world? These mysteries generate a mild form of suspense, while providing pretexts for spatial mobility.

Compared with the eccentric, almost fantastic plots of *Delicatessen* and *La Cité des enfants perdus*, *Amelie* adopts a more traditional approach, focusing on the exploration of different paths to love and happiness. The film is designed as a jigsaw with Amélie as the central piece, calling to mind the literary construction device used in Georges Perec's novel *La Vie mode d'emploi*, in which a Parisian block of flats and its residents serve as a pretext for multiple narratives and puzzle games.[3] Amélie is surrounded by a gallery of colourful, if undeveloped, characters who constitute the pieces of the jigsaw of her world, which will, once they are in place, enable her to sort out her own life.

Amélie's self-discovery journey includes various schemes that she develops in order to help others. She stimulates her father's desire to travel by having postcards of his missing garden gnome sent to him from tourist spots around the world; she acts as a matchmaker between Georgette and Joseph at the café by initiating their love affair; she comforts the concierge Madeleine Wallace with a fake letter from her late husband; she avenges

Lucien by disturbing Collignon's routine and making him believe that he is going mad; she copies the lines of the unpublished writer Hipolito on a street wall to boost his self-confidence. More importantly, Amélie emerges from her reserve and isolation to meet new people, especially Dufayel, with whom she has intimate conversations that gradually force her to open up. These help her to let go of her fantasy world, and it is the painter who eventually pushes her to confront her real life.

The film combines the familiar and the quaint, because it associates the local and the universal, the exotic and the ordinary. It lingers on the small aspects of everyday life to which everyone can relate, which have been identified by Michelle Scatton-Tessier as characteristic of 'petisme' (paying homage to little things and pleasures).[4] For example, Jeunet's film is a synaesthetic celebration of the sensorial as a mode of identification. Amélie is identified by colours (red and green), a musical theme (an accordion waltz), and simple, sensorial, pleasures, which are difficult to represent cinematically, some tactile as feeling grain or smooth flat pebbles, others olfactory, as in the reference to the ripe melons during the blind man's tour. These sensorial allusions anchor the film within the French 'air du temps', and can be linked to recent cultural trends, namely the unexpected success of books and songs which focus on ordinary characters and praise the simple pleasures, the most famous example being Philippe Delerm's successful collection of short stories *La Première Gorgée de bière et autres plaisirs minuscules*.[5] Moreover, objects are assigned a number of symbolic values: the marshmallow mixing machine at the end of the film points at time circularity, the stuffed dog in the concierge house at death, the numerous cameras at voyeuristic tendencies, and the garden gnome at Amélie's impish disposition.

Recycled audiovisual material is sometimes integrated into the narrative. For instance, in the prologue, an accelerated shot elliptically evokes Amandine Poulain's pregnancy, and the football game footage is used to prefigure the resourceful disposition of Amélie as a child. Other borrowed clips, such as the horse interrupting the Tour de France, the swimming-babies ballet and the man with the wooden leg, are not meant to fulfil any particular narrative function, but act as interludes, illustrating the quaintness of the film. These are complemented with pastiche scenes shot by Jeunet, going from the pseudo-retro photo novel of Amélie's memorial tribute, to brief frantic dramas recalling Jeunet's early short films, such as Nino's adventures in Afghanistan.

Linking visual style and narrative, a plethora of original ideas and surprises punctuate and enrich the script, as the episodes recounting the death of Amélie's mother, and her 'encounter' with Nino through the glass partition in the café, illustrate. With their varied genres and styles, these contribute to the heterogeneity of the film and the fragmentation of the narrative. In this respect, the opening credits sequence, directly incorporated into the narrative within the prologue, is a case in point. Revisiting a strategy already utilised in *Delicatessen*, it evokes the fantasy of Amélie's playful child world to introduce the technical crew. Each member is identified with suggestive props or visual elements associated with the function credited on the screen – for example, thick-lens glasses for the photographer, a five franc coin for the producer, and a wooden ruler for the editor.

The 20-minute prologue constitutes an unusual narrative gamble that sets the tone for the film. Covering a period of 24 years and commentated by an omniscient narrator in voiceover, it contains over 300 separate shots and intricate editing. It includes an accumulation of surreal vignettes designed to capture the audience's attention, which prompted the following comment from Dudley Andrew: 'At such rate each shot must make its impact instantly. This means that there can be no extraneous action in the frame, no competing visual features – one idea per shot being [Jeunet's] motto.'[6] It also implements, early on, a perception of the film-watching process as a form of image consumption.

From the first shot, the prologue fulfils the double function of contextualising the narrative and seducing the spectator. The first part retraces the important episodes of Amélie's childhood from her conception in 1973, introduces the main protagonists and highlights the whimsical, playful side of the film. Amélie's social isolation and withdrawn temperament are immediately attributed to the lack of affection that she received as a child. As Scatton-Tessier rightly notes, 'In Amélie's family, contact with others either induces stress, embarrassment or disappointment.'[7] In the second part, the prologue explicitly situates the adult Amélie in the main narrative time of 1997, and presents her circle of relations and her domestic circumstances.

The prologue also introduces Jeunet's distinctive fictional world and his personal vision of cinema. It acts as a summary of his filmography and a metaphor of his working method. For example, it contains a series of gags, illustrating his taste for complex mechanical devices and chain reactions, such as the TV aerial manipulation, or the lifting of the washing machine to retrieve the suicidal goldfish. The viewers who have seen his other films instantly recognise familiar elements at work, such as the use of wide-angle lenses and deforming close-ups, the old-fashioned sets and the accumulation of quaint objects. The shots featuring rooftops and the comic reference to the number of simultaneous orgasms in Paris both point at scenes from *Delicatessen*.

Finally, the prologue identifies the recurrent motifs, vignettes and visual idiosyncrasies, which will define the characters throughout the film. For example, Amélie is associated with naivety and imagination. As a child, she used to invent imaginary friends, believed that LPs were made like pancakes and that her camera was responsible for the accidents taking place in the world. As a young adult, she retains a vivid imagination, and indulges in the reassuring, simple pleasures of everyday life such as putting her hand in a sack full of grain, breaking the surface of her 'crème brûlée' with a spoon and skimming pebbles on the canal.

Time and space

Amelie rests upon a few precise temporal and spatial markers, which lend a sense of authenticity to the film. The key moments of the narrative are precisely dated and the Parisian locations are identified. After the prologue, the story begins in Amélie's Montmartre flat on 30 August 1997, an emblematic date in the public consciousness. On hearing of the death of Princess Diana on television, Amélie inadvertently drops a perfume cap and discovers a box of childhood treasures dating from the 1950s in the cavity of her bathroom wall. Feeling nostalgic, she sets herself a challenge to return it to its owner, and starts an investigation to find him, which will put her in contact with members of her local community, the caretaker, the grocer and his parents and, more importantly, the reclusive painter who will play an active role in her destiny. The scene is narrated in voiceover, adopting an omniscient viewpoint. Amélie remains silent, but the narrator interprets her actions and reactions, highlighting the dramatic importance of the scene and channelling the spectator's reaction.

Except in the reference to Diana's death, however, the film deliberately sends mixed spatial and temporal messages. Although precise times, dates and places are given, every effort seems to be made to re-create an undefined retro atmosphere. The first shot of the film exemplifies this ambiguity of space and time. It sets the film firmly in the real Montmartre, in the Rue Saint-Vincent to be precise. However, for many French viewers, this street also evokes a legendary cultural heritage, associated with the famous cabaret 'Le lapin agile', the lyrics of the popular song 'La complainte de la butte', written by Jean Renoir for his film *French Cancan* (1955), retracing the history of the Moulin Rouge.

Similarly, the strategy that consists of introducing the characters using their likes and dislikes projects them into a timeless world removed from reality. It is worth noting that Amélie's imagination plays an important part in the construction of this retro world, as is apparent when she dreams of herself on television as a heroic character replicating at once Louise Brooks's 1920s style and Mother Theresa, with a voiceover commentary made by the real-life television journalist Frédéric Mitterrand. As will be discussed more fully in Chapter Three, the amalgam of cultural and visual references from different periods reinforces this temporal and spatial ambivalence. Time seems to have stopped in the Montmartre of *Amelie*. Even the precise temporal markers provided by the narrator and the recurring shots of clocks that punctuate the narrative confuse the time issue, by adding superfluous information. They highlight the near-obsessive punctiliousness of the narrative, and mimic Jeunet's self-conscious approach to film-making.

Time and space in *Amelie* are marked by circularity. Life seems to be static or structured around repetitive actions. Amélie visits her father every weekend; she identifies with the girl with the glass in a Renoir painting that was made over 100 years ago, but that crucially is being remade every year by Dufayel; Nino works at the Foire du Trône every Wednesday, and he is repeatedly seen picking up pieces of photographs; Joseph seems to live in the café and spends his time recording conversations and playing them back endlessly; Lucien makes regular delivery rounds to the local customers and the grocer wakes up at the same time every day to open his shop. Even the emblematic images of the merry-go-round and the repetitive waltz motifs of the soundtrack point at circularity.[8]

The epilogue provides a good illustration of the circularity motif. Having just watched a video provided by Dufayel, Amélie realises that she must find Nino, and, as she opens the door, there he stands. In a fluid circular movement, the camera envelops them as they kiss. The film ends cheerfully, with Nino and Amélie riding round Paris on Nino's scooter, reminding the audience of Gregory Peck and Audrey Hepburn's sightseeing in *Roman Holiday* (William Wyler, 1953). Despite the brisk editing of the final ride, which suggests movement, freedom and new beginnings, Amélie's world remains rather static and self-contained.

It follows that, if a number of emblematic time and space markers initially provide an illusion of authenticity, a closer analysis shows that these are unreliable. They contribute more to enhancing the fantasy of the film, than to inscribing the narrative within a precise spatial and temporal context. This deliberate blurring of these two parameters as well as the generic heterogeneity discussed in the next section prefigure the postmodern quality of the film.

Amelie's genres and motifs

Genre hybridity

Amelie skilfully blends different genres, combining universal conventions associated with Hollywood cinema (romantic comedy and melodrama) with the more specifically French cultural and cinematic legacy of *cinéma du look* and Poetic Realism. Bringing together a feel-good atmosphere, a touch of fantasy, as well as other elements of comedy, the film can also be viewed as a modern fable, along the traditional lines of a quest for love and happiness.

Amelie's wide appeal can partly be attributed to its adoption of the conventions of romantic comedy, characterised by a happy ending and the ideal of romantic love. The focus is placed on a young heroine trapped in a lonely urban lifestyle, whose experience recalls that of characters played by Meg Ryan in *Sleepless in Seattle* (Nora Ephron, 1993) and Julia Roberts in *Notting Hill* (Roger Michell, 1999). These films, like *Amelie*, evoke a sense of local community, against which the romantic plot unfolds. Also typical is the way in which obstacles are placed in Amélie's path to delay the formation of the romantic couple.

In *Amelie*, romantic comedy is associated with melodrama, a genre characterised by 'excess, sensation, spectacle and affect, while assuming ethical emotions and fantasy solutions, and focusing on the exploration of personal history and identity',[9] which can all be traced in the film. Melodrama often induces nostalgia, thus becoming 'the form both to register change and to process change, in particular mediating relations between a lost but problematic past and the present'.[10] Through its problematic relation to time, sense of loss and the reluctance of the character to process change, *Amelie* adopts certain conventions of melodrama to represent nostalgia, a point discussed further in Chapter Three.

Poetic Realism

While romantic comedy and melodrama are 'universal' genres, *Amelie* also embraces the French cinematic legacy more specifically, by appropriating some of the conventions of the Poetic Realism of the 1930s, which combines naturalism and lyrical stylisation in stories set in 'popular' areas of Paris.[11] Jeunet has repeatedly expressed his admiration for the films of Marcel Carné and screenwriter Jacques Prévert, the most famous exponents of French Poetic Realism.[12] He also re-read Jacques Prévert's books, which then influenced the writing of *Amelie*: 'The reference to Prévert was constant. His vision is so poetic and surreal! He also makes lists and collects things. His work is a collection of magical words... That's exactly what I was aiming at.'[13] Given that Prévert's traditional themes include 'innocent love, societal repression, hypocrisy, fate and the triumph of the imagination',[14] it is easy to relate him to Jeunet's motifs.

The films of Poetic Realism are noted for polished witty dialogue, use of popular stars, sense of detail, and outstanding set reconstructions. Jeunet particularly referred to Carné's films *Quai des Brumes/Port of Shadows* (1938), featuring Jean Gabin and Michèle Morgan, *Hotel du Nord* (1938), starring Louis Jouvet and Arletty, and *Le Jour se lève/Daybreak* (1939), with Jean Gabin and Arletty. He asked his team to view these before shooting, and to pay special attention to the extraordinary sets created by Alexandre Trauner. On a more anecdotal note, Amélie had originally been named Garance after the heroine of *Les Enfants du Paradis* (Marcel Carné, 1942–1945), interpreted by Arletty.

Beyond a special attention paid to the small details and objects of daily life, the Poetic Realism of the 1930s portrayed working-class and petit bourgeois characters, in an attempt to represent 'reality' against the prevailing tradition of bourgeois dramas and comedies. Similarly, *Amelie* focuses on such 'ordinary' people and assigns significance to period objects and the small details of the past (sweets, posters, shop windows, furniture).

In the light of Jeunet's appropriation of some Poetic Realism motifs, it is necessary to clarify a few connections. In Carné's films, as in *Amelie*, destiny ruled the narrative and had a hold over characters' lives.[15] However, in classic Poetic Realism, the ideal of love and happiness was powerful yet usually doomed, in sharp contrast with the optimistic, dreamy tone of *Amelie* and its fairytale ending. The 1930s films were shot entirely in studios, thereby recreating a mythologised Paris, which was a very specific amalgam of minute realism and bold stylisation. Even if *Amelie* was shot largely on location, it stylises and manipulates the décor, in this instance to re-create retro images evoking the atmosphere of Poetic Realism more than its ideological backdrop. This décor is used as setting for surreal situations, transforming the Poetic Realism of the 1930s into a more hybrid 'poetic surreality'.

Surrealist motifs

'Surreal' is a term often used to describe Jeunet's early films. However, the word is more likely nowadays to mean unusual, bizarre or supernatural (in French 'décalé') than to refer to the Surrealist movement. *Amelie* is more anchored in verisimilitude than other examples of Surrealist cinema, as it does not aim to be experimental or provocative. However, Jeunet's playfulness and inventiveness may at times recall Surrealist motifs, often deployed to poetic effect. For example, the on-screen, non-diegetic information overlaid on the image with red arrows is an unconventional intervention into the picture and narrative, present in surrealist art.

The film also resorts to literal visual representations of linguistic idioms. The metaphorical expressions 'being love-struck', 'melting into tears' and 'seeing the light' are graphically illustrated on screen. Amélie literally melts into a water puddle in the café after Nino's departure, and her bright throbbing heart is graphically visualised when she first meets him in the station. Similarly, the blind man experiences a heart-warming feeling when a halo of light descends upon him after his meeting with Amélie. Using special effects, Jeunet creates spectacular images that can be considered Surrealist in spirit, but which have also been exploited in recent films, for example those of Quentin Tarantino, and television series such as *Ally McBeal*.

Another strategy recalling Surrealism involves visualising the characters' thoughts or daydreams by showing these on screen using various devices. These include the animation of objects (the bedside lamp), paintings (the animals in the bedroom pictures) and photographs (the man on the passport photographs telling Nino about Amélie). This is not dissimilar to a strategy used in Buñuel's *L'Age d'or* (1930), in which the man's fantasising about his lover is expressed by animating photographs in the shop window.

Composite superimposed images also serve to illustrate the dialogue in the scene between Amélie and Eva in the sex shop: Eva explains Nino's incongruous hobbies, including collecting footprints in cement and recordings of funny laughs, and impersonating Father Christmas. Simultaneously visual illustrations of these appear on screen (as in Amélie's mind), indicating how alike she and Nino are. More generally, the visual style of the film resorts to numerous tricks, gimmicks and special effects discussed in Chapter Three, which may evoke the Surrealist artists, such as literally drawing shapes in clouds in the fashion of Magritte's bright skies, or introducing visual dream sequences recalling the work of Salvadore Dali or Luis Buñuel.[16]

Fairytale and magical realism

I have argued that *Amelie* incorporates elements of romantic comedy and melodrama, Poetic Realism and Surrealist influences. This thus elicits a very hybrid generic identity, emblematic of postmodern cinema. Comments made by both critics and audiences often link the film to the literary genre of fairytales, partaking in a recent trend of French films inspired by children's classics.[17] Yet, while the world of *Amelie* is magical, its plot is not supernatural. It is a world filled with wonders, where everything seems possible: objects and photographs come to life and discuss the action; clouds adopt the reassuring shapes of cuddly toys; a street prompter suggests witty comments; and personal dreams are broadcast on television. In this respect, Amelie adheres to recent trends of mainstream cinema that refer back to childhood memories and tales, blending the real world with fantasy. It can be associated with such successes as the *Harry Potter* and *Shrek* series, but also with *Sleepy Hollow* (Tim Burton, 1999), *Le Grand Bleu* and, more generally, most of Steven Spielberg's films.

Delicatessen and *La Cité des enfants perdus* had drawn their inspiration from the darker side of children's fairytales. As for *Amelie*, it is specifically associated with *Little Red Riding Hood*, and Philomène, the air hostess, is nicknamed Blanche-Neige (Snow White) in reference to her carrying the garden gnome with her on her travels. Yet, there are no witches, no real signs of evil here. *Amelie* favours a more reassuring fantasy narrative than Jeunet and Caro's previous films,[18] and the characters seem to come straight out of innocent cartoons: the doe-eyed, pixie-like Amélie and the charismatic Lucien, a vulnerable victim one minute, and the next a conjurer who, like a fairy godmother, can transform a boring grocery delivery into a treat of caviar, foie gras and champagne.

These references to fantasy worlds point to the postmodern conventions of 'magical realism', defined in the 1980s by Fredric Jameson as 'the poetic transformation of the object world – not so much a fantastic narrative, then, as a metamorphosis in perception and things perceived'.[19] This transformation can be achieved by entering the characters' inner world (here Amélie's fantasy world), and also via production design including décor, costume and colour. Magical realism is also characterised by a return to a village/community culture and by the prevalence of imaginary solutions over real-world contradictions. These conventions are employed to some extent in *Amelie*, where production design is given special attention, and the local community plays an important role in the resolution of the plot. Amélie's inability to confront the real world is often assuaged by her taking refuge in her imagination.

Because it mixes different genre conventions, *Amelie* is sometimes perceived as a late product of the *cinéma du look* of the 1980s, but it is probably more relevant to link the film with the postmodern trends found in the French cinema of the 1980s and 1990s. More importantly, *Amelie*'s generic hybridity is central to the construction of Jeunet's cinema. Not only does his plural genre approach produce an original vision of the world, but it also reinforces the national identity of the film by accumulating powerful symbols of the French cultural heritage.[20] In addition, the genre analysis of *Amelie* can partly explain its popular success, because hybrid films are likely to appeal to a wider audience.

Other recurring motifs

The hybrid nature of *Amelie* encourages the exploration of a variety of themes and motifs including confinement, loss, loneliness and solidarity. Throughout the film there is a tension between confinement and movement. As Batiste Roux has noted, boxes (toy boxes, photo booths, cameras, photo frames), cavities and other places of confinement abound in the film. They translate Amélie's fear of confronting the outside world: 'In fact the whole film seems to be constructed around the motive of cavity, of the receptacle, which contributes to the balance and safety within the space [of the film].'[21] These boxes and cavities tend to generate a reassuring sense of safety rather than a feeling of claustrophobia.

However, Amélie's curiosity and her taste for convoluted schemes push her out of the safety of her confinement and force her to confront the real world. This involves travelling around Paris, frequenting public places and contacting people that she does not know. Gradually, Amélie ventures out more, first ensuring that she cannot be seen and recognised, or that she is out of reach. As the failed attempts to trace Dominique Bretodeau illustrate, she feels safer using a call-box than having to knock on people's doors. It is only once she forms a couple with Nino that she can dominate space and fully express her freedom. This tension between confinement and movement affects other characters: Amélie's recluse father is going to travel the world, which in a sense will allow her to emancipate herself from his depressing influence.

Although *Amelie* may appear to promote such values as friendship, solidarity and romantic love, it also lends itself to a less optimistic reading. As Michelle Scatton-Tessier rightly remarks, the film does not present the usual concerns of the average person of 2001 (employment, security, economic welfare), yet the narrative and characterisation contexts are not idealised:

'[B]elow the surface lies a plot preoccupied with angst, isolation, loss, sickness and death and a myriad of dysfunctional and lonely neighbours including a recluse, an alcoholic and a hypochondriac.'[22]

The characters all portray different visions of loneliness in our atomised society and, to a large extent, they have lost contact with their community, thus contradicting the assumption that *Amelie* functions as pure nostalgia. The visual style of the film may well encourage a nostalgic reading (see Chapter Three), but, under its surface idealised village microcosm, the narrative points at our technological society.[23] However, the characters' loneliness is more circumstantial than voluntary, and they are happy to cooperate when solicited in an exercise of solidarity. Madeleine Wallace is willing to help Amélie as it gives her the chance to confide in her, Collignon's parents do provide her with information, and Dufayel invites her in on his own initiative.

The much-publicised altruistic theme of the film, built around helping others and changing their lives, is ambivalent. Isabelle Daunais is not the only one to interpret Amélie's initiative to help other as peremptory and unduly manipulative.[24] It could be argued that the heroine's interference is not only reprehensible (she breaks into Collignon's flat and borrows the concierge's letters), but also hard to legitimise from a privacy perspective. From a moral viewpoint, her behaviour can also be questioned, as the happiness she causes is based on deceit (the concierge's husband did not write the letter, Georgette and Joseph were thrown into each other's arms rather than fell in love). However, as Scatton-Tessier argues, 'Amélie does not really transform people herself; she propels them backwards, providing a necessary distance for them to reconsider their existence so that closure and behaviour change may take place.'[25] For example, she does not directly lead Bretodeau to renew links with his family, rather this comes as a result of his childhood memories resurfacing. Amélie's schemes also induce her own transformation. In the process of helping others to review their situations, she starts looking at her own life.

Any debate about Amélie as a manipulator calls for the questioning of the film itself as a form of manipulation. The interfering trait of Jeunet's fairytale-like character in a fantasy film may seem insignificant compared to the manipulative streak of a film-maker who makes full use of the cinematic medium to create his own dream world. One thing is certain: in the process a charismatic and iconic character was created, which has already found its place in French cinema's portrait gallery.

Amélie Poulain: the creation of an iconic character

From the start, the viewers are under the impression of knowing Amélie inside out. They witness her conception and birth, then are given a lengthy audio-visual summary of her childhood and formative years, using a combination of voiceover commentary and flashbacks to explain the idiosyncrasies of her adult character, emotional state and fertile imagination. By the time the story really begins, they are aware of her unusual family background, her routine, tastes, fears and dreams, in a narrative strategy later reproduced concisely for the other characters.

Depicted as enchanting, and living in a fantasy world, Amélie seems to come from a cartoon or a fairytale. Rather than a 1990s Parisian young woman, she resembles in turn Olive Oyle in the Abbesses metro station scene, Alice in Wonderland as a little girl who lives in an imaginary world, and Little Red Riding Hood because of her red clothes. Moreover, the film explicitly refers to an iconic real-life princess (Lady Diana), with whom Amélie clearly identifies, and whom she tries to emulate.

Look and performance

Audrey Tautou's physical appearance, charm and performance style are crucial to her credibility in the part of Amélie. However, her distinctive look in the film is mainly the result of Jeunet's imagination and filming strategies. A closer look at the drawings made for the film's storyboard and the auditions included in the DVD proves revealing. The construction of Amélie involved remodelling Tautou's features. The sculptured bob haircut enhanced her face and smile, it brought out her ears, contributing to her being compared to a whimsical elf and a waif. Her wide 'Bambi' eyes were highlighted by close-ups and the use of wide-angle shots, which caused a slight distortion of features and emphasised her resemblance to a cartoon character. Jeunet had originally thought of bringing Amélie's hair up in a bun to show her nape, but he realised in the tests that her hairstyle had to be more structured[26] to achieve a more striking graphic look, and enhance the fantasy associated with the character.

Careful attention was paid to Amélie's costumes. She wears fitted, retro-style jackets, long lace skirts and low-neck tops and an old-fashioned slip. The femininity associated with lace is, however, cancelled by clumpy shoes worn with socks. Moreover, Amélie likes wearing disguises, as though her clothes helped her to hide and create new identities for herself. The headscarf that she wears at the carousel recalls Audrey Hepburn, to whom Tautou is often compared and after whom she was apparently named;[27] the Zorro costume in the photo album is yet another reference to popular cartoon and TV characters. Her colour schemes are not innocent either, a combination of red, apple green and brown, which for a start highlights her dark hair and eyes. The use of colour is analysed in detail in Chapter Three, yet from a characterisation viewpoint, the combination of red and green evokes Christmas, and the earthy brown not only contributes to her blending into the nostalgic sepia sets and going unnoticed, it also enhances her child-like world.

Child-woman or typical adulescent of the 1990s

Although a young woman of 23 in the film, Amélie shows clear signs of immaturity, wallowing in eternal adolescence. In this respect, she may be seen as a product of the 1990s generation of young adults who do not want to grow up, which French psychoanalyst Tony Anatrella referred to from the late 1980s as 'adulescents', a contraction of adult and adolescent.[28] Similarly, in a more recent study of 'adulescence', journalist Marie Giral sees the refusal to enter the adult world as a form of regressive behaviour that characterises Western societies in the late 1990s and the early 2000s, the diegetic time of *Amelie* and that of its production respectively.[29]

Adulescent behaviour takes different forms, all of which recall Amélie's world. Favouring playful activities and instant pleasures, it places excessive significance on the objects and dress codes of childhood. As Giral notes, contemporary television programmes and films mirror this social trend. Using French and American case studies, she singles out *Amelie* as an example of a reassuring and consensual film that presents immature characters with whom she feels, rather paradoxically given her general argument, that it is impossible to identify.[30] As Chapter Four will show, the reception of *Amelie* strongly contradicts Giral's reading. Many viewers did identify with the heroine, so much so that she became an icon and a social phenomenon.

Indeed, as argued by Ginette Vincendeau, Amélie represents a reassuring, familiar type of femininity: the femme-enfant (child-woman).[31] She amalgamates the child-woman characters from Jeunet's other films. Her body is slightly androgynous, tomboyish, and timeless outfits conceal her curves, emphasising her gamine look. She thus recalls other such figures in French

Figure 3: Amelie's bedroom.

cinema in recent years, including Juliette Binoche, Charlotte Gainsbourg and Sylvie Testud.

For reasons similar to those discussed by Ginette Vincendeau in relation to Binoche in her early films,[32] Amélie/Tautou represents a non-threatening, romanticised form of femininity, which can to some extent explain her wide appeal with audiences of all ages and social backgrounds (see Chapter Four). She fantasises about the number of orgasms in Paris at a given time, but her own sexuality is dormant, and she longs for conventional fairytale romance. As psychoanalyst Sylvia Salgo notes, 'Amélie is an adult who avoids sexuality. She tries to keep her life within the world of childhood pleasures, notably through playing games.'[33] Although she is no longer a child, her attitude shows that she is scared of stepping into an adult world, and that, borrowing Batiste Roux's words, her character is 'articulated around the trauma of lost childhood'.[34]

In the early stages of the film, Amélie is inhibited. She enjoys being around people, but is pathologically shy and withdrawn, to the point of sometimes becoming transparent, as is evident in the scene when she first meets Nino at the station, or on her encounter with Bretodeau in the bar, where she chokes in her drink because he addresses her directly. She prefers mediated communication through videotapes, fliers, cryptic notes, photographs or anonymous phone calls.

As the film progresses, however, she gradually becomes the driving force of the action, orchestrating her schemes single-handed. Paradoxically, the more she interferes, the more she lives her life through other people. As the legendary character of 'Zorro', whose costume she borrows on two occasions, she becomes a 'justicière' (an avenger of wrong), whose ethical legitimacy is questionable because of the voyeurist nature of her activities.[35] Amélie watches her neighbours with a telescope, but this is to fill her lonely life, not for sexual reasons as is often the case for voyeurs. As part of her schemes, she often sees without being seen, but again this is a symptom of her pathological shyness, not of perverse tendencies. The voyeur in cinema is usually associated with male characters, and Amélie is not convincing as a female voyeur. This probably explains why her voyeuristic penchants are not perceived as threatening. Like the romantic approach to her (non-existent) sexuality, her voyeurism is infantilised and reduced to playing (hide-and-seek) games.

Gender and iconicity

Arguably, Amelie portrays a rite of passage, a coming of age, from childhood to adulthood, from dreamland to the 'real' world. Jeunet had briefly considered a male protagonist, possibly played by Mathieu Kassovitz, before setting his mind on a young woman. He made the right decision. A male protagonist would fail to make the same impact, because, as Vincendeau has argued, 'the fantasy that Amélie represents is gendered':

Her primary fantasy role is that of the good fairy – projected on to a variety of contemporary 'caring' women from Diana, Princess of Wales, to Mother Theresa [...]. She exists to satisfy others, and it's difficult to imagine a man cast in this role [...]. Amélie had to be a woman because of her emblematic function. [...] her femininity is a blank page on which others' fantasies can be inscribed.[36]

Amélie is a reassuring image of innocence, rather than its flesh and bone incarnation. She is iconic of a certain form of French femininity (slightly unreal gamine as opposed to sex kitten). She is also a media icon in more than one sense, as Elisabeth Ezra has argued: in the diegesis, the character sees her image on television, and Amélie's face has also travelled all round the world on the film's posters. Her iconicity is linked to performance: she is at once accessible and unreal, hence ordinary but out of reach.[37]

In developing a character type already present in Jeunet's previous films, Amélie comes to represent the female double of the director, reflecting to an extent his own state of mind and preoccupations. More crucially, thanks to Tautou, she benefits from extraordinary screen presence, and her charismatic face and personality play a major role in the success of the film. She also blends fully with the gallery of secondary characters, which surround her and contribute to create a typical Jeunet microcosm of likeable eccentric people.

Nino, Amélie's charming prince and alter-ego, is described as 'goofy, kooky and adorable',[38] and he too comes out as eccentric and surreal. Like Amélie, Nino was a solitary child, before turning into an immature adult who works in a sex shop, when he is not the skeleton in the ghost train of the Foire du Trône. One of his many hobbies is to collect discarded photographs in Photomats and carefully file them in an album.

In considering the narrative heterogeneity of *Amelie*, its generic hybridity, motifs, numerous cinematic influences and characterisation, this chapter has uncovered a series of typical traits of postmodern cinema, which will be explored further in the next chapter devoted to Jeunet's distinctive cinematic style.

Notes

1   For a more detailed discussion of *fait divers* in *Amelie*, see M. Scatton-Tessier: 'Le Petisme' 2004, pp.205–206.

2   It is ironic that there is doubt as to her real identity: some specialists think that it is the actress Ellen Andrée while others, including Renoir's son Jean, opt for a model known as la belle Angèle.

3   Paris: Larousse, 1978.

4   Scatton-Tessier: 2004, pp.197–207.

5   Paris: Gallimard, 1997. For examples of popular songs, see young artists like Bénabar and Vincent Delerm.

6   D. Andrew, 'Amélie or le fabuleux destin du cinéma français', *Film Quarterly* 57: 3, p.41.

7   Scatton-Tessier: 2004, p.200.

8   See P. Powrie, 'The fabulous destiny of the accordion in French cinema', in P. Powrie and R. Stilwell (eds), *Changing Tunes: The Use of Pre-existing Music in Film* (Aldershot: Ashgate, 2006), pp. 146-150, for a more detailed analysis of the repetitive music.

9   J. Bratton, J. Cook and C. Gledhill (eds), *Melodrama: Stage, Picture, Screen* (London: BFI, 1994), pp.1–2.

10   Bratton, Cook and Gledhill: 1994, p.2.

11   There is no space to develop the analysis of Poetic Realism, which has been studied and defined elsewhere, for example in D. Andrew's works: 'Poetic Realism', M.L. Brandy (ed.) *Rediscovering French Film* (New York: Museum of Modern Art, 1983), and *Mists of Regret: Culture and Sensibility in Classic French Film* (Princeton: Princeton University Press, 1995). I focus here on selected aspects relevant to *Amelie*.

12   Jeunet singles out Marcel Carné's visual style as a source of inspiration in E. Libiot, 'Le musée imaginaire de Jean-Pierre Jeunet: que du cinéma,' *L'Express*, 1 November 2004. Caro had already paid tribute to the films of this period at the time of *Delicatessen*; see Bernard: 1991, p.81.

13   M. Marvier, 'Jean-Pierre Jeunet le collectionneur', *Synopsis* 13 (May–June 2001), pp.52–55 (p.55). See also Jeunet's tribute to Prévert's distinctive poetic world in Libiot: 2004, and the analysis of Prévert references in *Amelie* in Andrew: 2004, p.38.

14   Andrew: 1995, p.75.

15   See chaos theory and fate intervention as discussed in the study of the prologue.

16   'Much of the film is shot in a haunting amber twilight straight out of Magritte', E. Abee, '*Amelie*', *Film Journal International*, 28 August 2002. The recurrent presence of clocks evokes Dali and the eye imagery is central to Surrealist cinema.

17   See, for example, *Les Amants criminels* (François Ozon, 1999), *Promenons-nous dans les bois* (Lionel Delplanque, 2000) and *Le Petit Poucet* (Olivier Dahan, 2001).

18   M. Giral, *Les Adolescents: Enquête sur les nouveaux comportements de la génération Casimir* (Paris: Le Pré aux clercs, 2002), p.56.

19   F. Jameson, 'On Magic Realism and Film', *Critical Enquiry* 12 (Winter 1986), p.301.

20   See R. Moine article 'Vieux genres? Nouveaux genres? Le fabuleux destin de quelques films français' (2004) for a more detailed discussion of how generic hybridity reinforces the national identity of the film.

21   B. Roux, 'Les vertiges de l'intimité', *Positif* 487 (September 2001), p.65.

22   Scatton-Tessier: 2004, p.199.

23   On this subject, see R.C. Moore's essay (2006), which analyses *Amelie*'s use of technology in relation to issues of freedom and power.

24   I. Daunais, 'Le grand jeu', *Inconvénient* 8 (February 2002), pp.67–74.

25   Scatton-Tessier: 2004: p.204.

26   Jeunet, Laurant and Desportes: 2004, p.8.

27   See for example *USA Today*'s review (Walt 2001).

28   T. Anatrella, *Interminables Adolescences: Les 12–30 ans* (Paris: Cerf/Cujas, 1988).

29   Giral: 2002, pp.55–56. See also recent films such as *Tanguy* (Chatiliez, 2001) and *L'Auberge espagnole/Pot Luck* (Klapisch, 2002), which illustrate 'adulescent' behaviour.

30   Giral: pp.55–56.

31   Vincendeau: 2001, p. 25. Vincendeau: 2005, pp. 12–16.

32   G. Vincendeau, *Stars and Stardom in French Cinema* (London: Continuum, 2000), p.243.

33   Quoted in M. Kandel, 'Les fabuleuses recettes d' "Amélie Poulain"', *Le Point*, 11 May 2001, p.76.

34   Roux: 2001, p.65.

35   See Daunais: 2002, pp.72–73.

36   Vincendeau: 2001, p.25.

37   Ezra: 2004, pp.303–304.

38   S. Jeffries, 'It's hard for me to play romantic. I come across as a bit of a jerk', *Guardian*, 6 August 2001.

3 Postmodern style and Jeunet's signature

'Jeunet has a knack for finding visual answers to narrative problems.'[1]

'I cannot understand why a film should be ugly to be moving.'
J.-P. Jeunet[2]

Anchored more in popular culture than in the literary or theatrical traditions, *Amelie* offers spectacular entertainment, and promotes a playful, yet perfectionist approach to film-making. Relying on meticulous preparation and coordinated production values, the film combines high-tech cinematography, elaborate *mise-en-scène* with a quaint retro atmosphere. This chapter analyses the aesthetic choices that characterise *Amelie*'s visual style, focusing on cinematography, the manipulation of colour, the role played by special effects, and discusses the use of sound and the evocative soundtrack. It argues that Jeunet's distinctive cinematic style not only embraces postmodern film-making trends, but also re-creates a timeless Paris, which has contributed to the success of the film.

Amelie's visual feast: *mise-en-scène* and special effects

The film combines lavish images and effective cinematography. The sets have been carefully colour-coordinated, and unsightly flaws have been deleted – there are no graffiti, or litter in *Amelie*'s Paris. In the early 1990s, *Delicatessen* had been acclaimed for its innovative, almost prototypical use of cinematography and technologies, which 'explode[d] the realistic principles of artistic representation,'[3] and *La Cité des enfants perdus* pioneered the use of new digital software for postproduction.

Jeunet often quotes three key cinematic influences to his style: (1) Sergio Leone's *Once Upon a Time in the West* (1968) for the playful side of film-making; (2) Stanley Kubrick and *A Clockwork Orange* (1971) as an aesthetic influence; (3) film animation for its potential to push back the limits of what is possible in cinema.[4] Considering that Leone's cinema is often labelled 'mannerist, baroque, spectacular, exhibitionist, performative, carnivalesque, camp, cartoonish, "pop formalist" – a cinema of effects rather than meanings, of playful excess rather than classical expressiveness',[5] it is easy to understand its appeal for Jeunet. Kubrick helped him to realise that cinema can use shot length, music or ellipsis to create stunning visual and sound effects.[6] And, finally, apart from its impact on characterisation, animation directly inspired the sets and visual freshness of the film. For instance, a number of dramatic devices and visual effects in *Amelie* recall the spirit of *Tex Avery* cartoons and Jacques Tardi's distinctive graphic style.

While revealing some continuity and coherence in the influences underpinning Jeunet's films, *Amelie* explores further the screen representation of fantasy, the transposition of animation and *bande dessinée* techniques to the cinema, and the application of a precise personal aesthetic project. The unusual imagery of the film, enhanced by the use made of state-of-the-art digital technology, confirms Jeunet's reluctance to 'reproduce the everyday reality without discrepancy ('décalage'), or to film what he doesn't like'.[7] This goes some way to explain the specific *mise-en-scène* strategies that contribute to the construction of his artistic signature.

Mise-en-scène *and composition*

Amelie's carefully composed images not only serve the semi-fantasy world of the film but also clarify the narrative. As a critic once noted, 'Jeunet has a knack for finding visual answers to narrative problems: for him, an image, be it for an instant, will always be more telling than dialogue'.[8] These visual answers comprise the use of still images to explain precise situations. For instance, through the mediation of the girl in the Renoir painting, Amélie is made to project her own emotional state onto the mysterious gaze of the young woman with the glass. Although occupying a central position in the painting, this character seems to be absent from its narrative, just as Amélie is central to the plot of the film, but appears lost and isolated. The painting is therefore overtly integrated into the *mise-en-scène* to convey information, and even to trigger the narrative progression, since it functions as a catalyst for the heroine's confessions to Dufayel.[9] However, in most cases, Jeunet's images complement rather than replace the dialogue (or the voiceover), in a display of surreal effects (see digital effects section).

A series of explicit core principles that inform Jeunet's approach to *mise-en-scène* are applied to *Amelie*. The first of these, often quoted in interviews, states that 'every shot should be composed like a painting'.[10] Specific pictorial influences are discussed in the section on colour, but the impact of the analogy with painting extends beyond evoking a painter's style or colour scheme. It affects the construction of each frame and imposes strict discipline during shooting. For all the artistic skill that this filming strategy demonstrates (elaborate editing and camera mobility), it also runs the risk of creating static, de-contextualised vignettes, which tend to encapsulate the characters in their fantasy world. For example, when Amélie blissfully walks across the Pont des Arts, the blurred background and use of slow motion contribute to the stylisation of the scene. However, in an earlier bird's-eye shot of her lying in bed, the zooming in, combined with a 360° movement of the camera, had brought an initially static image to life, suggesting the heroine's inner turmoil.

Because of Jeunet's animation background, it is not surprising to find that the second principle should emphasise the graphic dimension of the image.[11] From the storyboard stage to the composition of the scenes, the frames are carefully chosen by the director himself, as are the intricate camera movements. There are many examples of fast-forward zooming recalling animation technique. Wide-angle lenses are preferred, and the camera is often placed near the ground or close to the actors. In addition to influencing the choice of set, the 25, 20 and 18mm focal lengths modify perspective and depth of field.[12] Not only do they distort the straight lines towards the edges of the frame, but they also exaggerate the distance between foreground and background planes, making the sets look more imposing, especially when the use of lighting preserves the definition of the background.

Wide-angle distortions are used for close-ups, in which faces fill the screen and appear to loom into the camera. Because the heightened perspective can make faces bulge in an unflattering way, Jeunet and his director of photography, Bruno Delbonnel, had to find the best-suited lens for Audrey Tautou's features. The result was convincing, as Amélie's distinctive close-ups not only stress her cartoon-like nature, but create a form of intimacy and favour a feeling of complicity between character and spectator. Moreover, as the actor's gaze is almost head-on into the lens, the camera becomes 'inquisitive, almost peering into the actor's soul'.[13]

Long focal lengths have occasionally been employed in the film to create a contrast in the few scenes when the characters look through binoculars – for example, as Dufayel observes Amélie from his flat, or when Nino catches a glimpse of Amélie at the Sacré-Coeur. In addition, crane shots, involving intricate camera movements and heavy equipment, enhance the impression of isolation, particularly in the scenes featuring Amélie in the station, or when she is skimming stones into the canal. A number of high-angle shots also contribute to provide an omniscient viewpoint on Amélie's actions, including spectacular bird's-eye shots, when she goes into the sex shop, near the carousel, or when she is reading the concierge's letters.

More generally, the camerawork illustrates a playful approach to film-making, reinforcing the light-hearted, cartoon-like tone of the film. A favourite technique involves camera tilting. Several shots start from a low angle in Orson Welles style, the camera gradually moving up to reveal a character, as is the case in the scenes with the mysterious red-shoed man, or when Nino is looking for photographs. Occasionally, the character enters the frame a few seconds after the shot has started, creating surprise effects recalling Sergio Leone. This is particularly effective when a fidgety Nino appears on the left side of the screen near the carousel below the Sacré-Coeur, unsure of what to expect, and again later, when he misses the appointment with Amélie in the station. In the latter, the complex camera movement ends on a close-up of his nape. Nino is clearly looking for something, and suddenly the camera captures his thoughts, embracing his point of view: he has recognised the red shoes in the booth.

Another playful manifestation of *mise-en-scène* is the use made of mirrors and glass. The numerous mirrors in the café, the glass partition on which Amélie writes the menu, and the train windows in which her face is repeatedly reflected all symbolically enhance her isolation. As for the frosted glass appearing in various scenes in the metro, the station and Dufayel's flat, it enhances elaborate lighting effects. Similarly, the diegetic use of the painter's video as he is filming Lucien enables a shot and reverse shot to be viewed in the same frame through the television screen.

The guiding principles and *mise-en-scène* strategies deployed in *Amelie* achieve more than a mere display of self-conscious expertise and mastery of the medium. By mimetically echoing narrative elements, they fully contribute to the construction of an inventive style that blends diverse influences and a personal vision of cinema. For example, a rotary 180° movement of camera is used to visualise Nino's surprise at discovering the identity of the man in the red shoes, literally turning his head upside down. The numerous special effects discussed below offer more illustrations of mimetic visualisation.

These strategies fully participate in the success of the film. They are at once innovative and effective, as the light-heartedness felt by audiences indicates. However, it must be emphasised that they promote film-making as a deliberate process of manipulation of images, in which effects are staged rather than captured on film, thus breaking away from the spontaneity values inherited from the New Wave (see Chapter One). Moreover, this type of cinematography cannot be dissociated from the use of digital technology, which is integrated into the *mise-en-scène* throughout the film.

'Interpretation and control': the potential of digital images

If special effects are not the primary trademark of French (and European) cinema, they were used effectively in a number of popular French films in 2001 to achieve a range of effects – enhance realism, create stunning imaginary worlds, or produce spectacular effects (see Table 2 in Appendix 2). In *Amélie*, 123 shots in total were manipulated in order to 'correct the sets, interpret reality and control images'.[14] The film was mainly shot on location, and then modified in postproduction to produce a semi-realist décor, which is not the same as creating and compositing entirely digital images.[15]

Amelie perpetuates a ten-year fruitful collaboration between Jeunet and the French special effects company Duboi.[16] It was they who developed digital software specifically designed for cinema, and were responsible for the special effects of the film as well as the digitisation work. The 'Dutruc' multiplatform software package, a 794,000-line special effect application with a paint tool, colour-chooser and cut-manager, was pioneered on *La Cité des enfants perdus*, and 'Duboicolor', designed in 2000, was tested with *Amelie*. In the same way as a colour printer, the latter combines the different technologies used for the digitisation process. It enables real-time colour-timing, the inclusion of superimposed images and special effects without losing the colour definition. These tools tackle the main digital processes used in *Amelie*, namely manipulation and grading of colour, insertion of special effects and editing.

'Cinematic impressionism': manipulating colour

Central to the aesthetic originality of *Amelie*, the use of colour forms part of a conscious directorial strategy, carefully orchestrated with the technical team. Bright use of colour enhances the 'feel-good' atmosphere of the film and its glowing visual style. It brings to mind in turn Tim Burton's atmospheric fairytales (*Batman* 1989, *Edward Scissorhands* 1990, *Sleepy Hollow* 1999), the surreal worlds of Terry Gilliam's *Brazil* (1985) and *12 Monkeys* (1995),[17] and the 1950s escapist Technicolor musicals of Vincente Minnelli. Strategies include contrasting saturated colours and sepia tones, as well as resorting to black and white for vintage newsreels (Tour de France), archival footage (the dancing one-legged man, the Russian film)[18] and Jeunet's own pastiche scenes (Amélie's memorial on television). The switch to black and white also signals certain incursions into the intimacy of the characters, as illustrated in the childhood flashbacks of Bretodeau and Nino, or in the visualisation of the characters' likes and dislikes.

The chromatic patterns of *Amelie* are directly inspired by paintings, drawing from a variety of styles and periods of figurative art, from Impressionism to contemporary artists. A familiar Renoir masterpiece of the Impressionist period, *Le Déjeuner des canotiers/The Luncheon at the Boating Party* (1881), plays a key role in the film. Apparently, this particular painting was chosen because it had a number of characters and interconnected gazes, which made it easy to imagine stories about them, but also, more pragmatically, because it was free of rights. Beyond the fact that Renoir lived in Montmartre, the essence of Impressionist art is to capture and represent happiness, which this painting exemplifies with its rich, warm colours. *Le Déjeuner des canotiers* thus has natural affinities with *Amelie*, and it is appropriated by the film through Dufayel's incessant attempts to recapture its characters' lives and looks, year after year. It thus comes to symbolise the creative process of the artist, and brings up the issue of visual signature.

Impressionist painting more generally has inspired the brightly-lit sets and warm colours of *Amelie*, especially in outdoor scenes. Furthermore, Jeunet's visual style has been described as 'cinematic impressionism',[19] in an attempt to link the digitally produced colours in his films with the distinctive techniques of Impressionism in painting, and also the avant-garde cinema of the 1920s.[20] Although this comparison may on first consideration seem excessive, a closer look at the film's images and sets reveals some striking coincidences, such as the fascination for recreating the light of station halls and the reflection of water in the canal (Claude Monet), Montmartre's cobbled streets (Toulouse-Lautrec) and its traditional cafés (Paul Cézanne).[21] However, it can be problematic to associate the naturalism underpinning Impressionist painting and a film with Jeunet's style in *Amelie* because of the overt manipulation of images and pastiche representation of Paris.

Another pictorial source of inspiration for *Amelie*'s visual style is Juarez Machado, a contemporary Brazilian painter whom Jeunet accidentally met in Montmartre.[22] In particular, his 'Hôtel Costes' series and the 'La fête continue' collection exhibited in 1997–1998 in Paris prompted the warm interior colour schemes of the film, mixing rich reds, oranges and browns.[23] Finally, although a less overt influence, the work of American painter Edward Hopper inspired certain angular suburban house façades, quaint staircases, as well as the use made of warm colours in some shots to enhance the depth of field.[24]

As the film poster prefigures, the dominant hues in *Amelie* are red and green, often complemented with golden yellow. Omnipresent in the film, red acts as a focal point within most frames, and a recurrent motif – for, among others, the dwarf's hat, the throbbing heart, the sex shop, the café's façade, the man's shoes, Amélie's clothes and her home. In her flat, the set-design blends warm shades of red and orange, creating a safe and cosy atmosphere. More generally, for other scenes shot indoors, red is combined with rich golden browns, often used in seemingly monochromatic tones, and suggesting a subtle retro atmosphere, not purely through sepia fading (the concierge's lodge and Dufayel's flat, the café and the stations). Brightly-lit golden hues also bring out many outdoor scenes, enhancing the light-hearted tone of the film.

If red is a recurring motif throughout the film, it is repeatedly contrasted with various shades of green, expressing different moods: the canal St Martin is depicted as a restful sun-lit green spot, while the glo-green effect in the metro scene with the blind man, the spooky fluo-green in the ghost-train, or the khaki tones in Collignon's flat suggest more eerie atmospheres. In addition, in Jeunet's colour chemistry, 'the gold and the green harmonise with the range of other colours, outside the range of traditional colour chemistry'.[25] In other words, an originality of the film is to combine tones that are not traditionally complementary. These combinations produce enchanting effects that enhance the innocence and simplicity of Amélie's world. They stimulate the imagination or trigger memories (Christmas decorations for example). Rich colours also bring out the cartoon and fairytale atmosphere, thus distinguishing *Amelie* from the gritty realism of a number of French films made in the 1990s. From a more technical perspective, if colour contrasts are facilitated by digital tools, their effectiveness also relies on the preliminary work done on set. This is particularly true of the scenes shot in the café, for example, with bright neon lights, warm hues and glittering copper bar, which all enhance the lively feel of the place. To ensure continuity of lighting, a canvas frame blocking out sunlight was placed outside the broad windows.[26]

Although some fine-tuning took place in postproduction, 90 per cent of the lighting effects were achieved during the main photography.[27] Just as all the colours had to appear on the rushes before they could be highlighted digitally, the light consistency could not be altered in postproduction.[28] This is why Delbonnel added filters to capture the expressiveness on the actors' faces, and control changes in natural light. Projectors were used to create different effects: in the ghost-train scene, for instance, the backlighting enhancing the cobwebs was combined with contrasting patches of light and dark to create a surreal atmosphere. For interior scenes, the possible loss of secondary hues in postproduction was anticipated by adapting the lighting: 'For the painter's flat, I systematically re-lit the blue tints or blue objects to preserve some of the secondary colour effects on film.'[29] Similarly, blue spots regularly appear in interior scenes, to add intensity – electric blue lampshades in Amélie's flat, and the blue television screen at Dufayel's.

The work on colour was completed in postproduction using digital timing processes (also called digital mastering or digital colour grading): 'We changed the skies, we put in clouds. I wanted an explosion of colour – the yellowish, Ektachrome-style look was part of my concept from the beginning.'[30] The entire film was digitally processed, which improved colour consistency and facilitated the insertion of the numerous special effects. The Duboi team

Figure 4: The ghost-train scene.

and the editor were often present on set to advise on the potential for postproduction modifications in relation to colour grading and lighting continuity and other effects. These manipulations produced a series of poetic, magical and symbolic effects, masking the boundaries between fantasy and the real world.

Colour was not just used for aesthetic purposes, but was also explored in the thematic content of the narrative, for instance through the painting motif. Dufayel and Lucien are associated with colour. The former endlessly copies the subtle tones of his master Renoir, himself recognised in his time as an innovator in his experimentation with colour. The latter, on the other hand, offers a more naive rendering using bright primary colours, which correspond to his infantile personality. The painting scenes at Dufayel's thus playfully mimic the work of Duboi's colourists and their computerised palette, metaphorically linking the work of the painter and that of the film-maker.

We have seen how digital colour adds expressiveness and chromatic continuity to the visual style of the film. Yet, by mixing sepia and saturated hues, it also blurs temporal markers, and favours a sense of timelessness often associated with postmodern cinema. This self-conscious use of colour revives the paradox of high technology serving a retro nostalgic visual style, which had been a distinctive feature of the *cinéma du look* of the 1980s. Similarly, *Amelie* contrasts colourful animation and advertising aesthetics with more monochromatic nostalgia. This helps to create a rich palette that draws its originality, and many would say 'poetic expressiveness', from hybrid influences (cinematic, photographic and pictorial), and a combination of skills blending traditional techniques and high-tech processes.

More generally, *Amelie* illustrates the significant changes in the treatment of colour in film in the digital age. Not only does it open up new possibilities, but it also extends directorial control to an aspect of film-making traditionally left to the technical crew, and adds another dimension to the concept of *mise-en-scène*. However, it must be stressed that digital colour grading remains an expensive process that significantly affects production values, and revives the debate around the relationship between art and financial considerations. The choice of digital technology conditions the artistic decisions made regarding colour effects, and becomes even more relevant in the case of special effects.

Digital magic: the special effects of Amelie

As illustrated in films as different as *Les Visiteurs* (Jean-Marie Poiré, 1993), *Forrest Gump* (Robert Zemeckis, 1994), *Pleasantville* (Gary Ross, 1998), *Le cinquième Élément* (Luc Besson, 1997) or *Titanic* (James Cameron, 1997), computer-generated imagery (CGI) can effectively enhance realism, create stunning fantasies or stage spectacular effects. It also facilitates the visual representation of magical and symbolic effects. In *Amelie*, digital special effects become an integral part of Jeunet's mode of representation, used 'to push back the limits of what is possible', and 'to renew the cinematic language'.[31] They become an additional source of inspiration and creative stimulation.

Before considering specific examples from *Amelie*, the classification devised by Christian Metz in the 1970s[32] can help to organise different types of special effects into three categories. The first category, 'visible effect', breaks the illusion of reality in favour of fantasy and spectacle. Examples of effects include 3D animations, morphings and warpings, which, in transforming and distorting shapes, complement the use of deforming short lenses. Metz then distinguishes between 'invisible tricks' that the viewers can sense but cannot explain, including blue-screened scenes, and composite shots merging several layers of images, and 'imperceptible effects' that can neither be seen, nor guessed unless they are disclosed. These include some mechanical effects, and digital processes such as deletion or touching-up.

Even in the digital age, it remains relevant to distinguish traditional 'mechanical special effects' or 'live mechanical tricks' realised during the shooting from 'digital visual effects' performed on computer in post-production. Both methods were combined in *Amelie*, requiring the presence of two distinct teams, Les Versaillais and Duboi, and implying a form of collaboration emblematic of Jeunet's style, namely the blending of reality and artifice, of craft and high tech.

Provided by Yves Domenjoud and his team, known as Les Versaillais,[33] the 15 mechanical effects include the floating glasses and tablecloth in the prologue, the crockery moving on the café shelves and the scene with the perfume cap in Amélie's bathroom. Elaborate systems involving fans, vibrators, invisible chutes and springs were deployed, highlighting a perfectionist attention to detail, as this account of the procedure for the bathroom scene confirms:

> With clockwork precision, the perfume cap escapes the hand of the heroine, bounces between her feet before hitting the skirting board of the bathroom. A tile falls off, revealing the hiding place of a child's treasure. This scene is full of tricks. The Plexiglas cap slides into a small chute, and goes straight into the tile. A device makes the tile vibrate until it falls off. For that scene alone there were several tests in a lab, one day of preparation in the studio and another for the shooting of the scene.[34]

Such elaborate operations find an echo in the film narrative: Amélie's revenge on Collignon involves devising similar mechanical schemes, such as tampering with electrical appliances. Her DIY schemes thus recall the various forms of 'bricolage' that also characterise the film-making process.

Duboi's digital special effects, supervised by Alain Simkine, comprise examples of Metz's three categories (see Table 3). Some shots were manipulated on a computer, for example integrating matte-paintings to filmed images to create animal-shaped clouds. Similarly, backgrounds were merged with blue-screened shots, when Amélie beholds Paris on the roof, for instance. These 'invisible effects' are purely aesthetic improvements, illustrating

Jeunet's taste for effects that last a few seconds. They all contribute to the sense of detail which characterises the film. As it was difficult to achieve seven bounces in front of the camera when skimming a stone on the canal, Amélie had a little help in postproduction thanks to the compositing technique. The ricochets in the water were reworked, so as to bounce at the right moment in line with the camera.[35]

In other cases, objects and characters were transformed and animated using visible special effects, providing visual answers to narrative requirements. The crocodile with which Amélie plays as a child is a 3D animation. The suicidal goldfish is really thrown into the water, but its reflection underwater is reconstructed digitally using the Maya 3D process to introduce an elusive sad expression in the close-up of the eye.[36] The animated paintings of the goose and the dog have been modelled into 3D, creating fantasy effects designed to bring a smile to the spectator's face. Because the main difficulty was to re-create the texture of the painting before animating it in 3D, this was done with a morphing.[37] A similar strategy was used for the pig of the lamp-base, which comes to life, talks and turns the light off when Amélie goes to sleep, thus introducing an extra narrative viewpoint.

The most spectacular examples of visible special effects are the supernatural animations borrowed from cartoon aesthetics, which enhance the magical nature of the film. They include the 'throbbing heart' and 'melting into tears' metaphors that literally visualise Amélie's emotions and dramatise ` turning the film into pure spectacle.

Table 2: Digital visual and special effects in *Amelie*

Type of effect	Number of occurrences found in *Amelie*	Selected examples
Blue-screened shots	15	Magpie at Amélie's father Nino in Afghanistan Amélie peering at the city's skyline Amélie and Nino on scooter
Composited shots	35 (including animations)	Visual illustrations of Nino's hobbies in sex shop e.g. Father Christmas ringing bell Amélie's dreamed life with Nino The four talking photographs
2D and 3D animations of objects	6 main ones	Sad-eyed goldfish Animated pig lamp The four animated photos

Type of effect	Number of occurrences found in *Amelie*	Selected examples
Computer-generated model objects or signs	5	Talking paintings of goose and dog Key visible through Amélie's clothes Crocodile toy Amélie's heart Superimposed inlays (arrows, text, etc.)
Morphing/warping	3 main ones	Blind man's happiness in halo Amélie's throbbing heart Amélie dissolving into tears
Matte paintings	12	Animal-shaped clouds Collignon's parents' house Garden gnome photographs Nino in Afghanistan
Accelerated shots	23	Credits scene Composition of caretaker's letter The overhead metro shot
[and]		Afghanistan montage Scooter ride, etc.
Slow-motion shots		Amélie on Pont des Arts Amélie as Zorro Bald man walking in station Ghost-train scene Lost marbles in school yard, etc.

Table 3: Metz's classification of special effects applied to Jeunet's films

	Visible effects	Invisible effects (not seen but guessed)	Imperceptible effects (neither seen nor perceived)
Technical live special effects	Live light effects (camera filters, artificial lighting)	Creation of **model** buildings or objects to replace real ones: wires, springs, vibrators or live	Invisible cables in the café Chute to direct the perfume cap's trajectory

	Visible effects	Invisible effects (not seen but guessed)	Imperceptible effects (neither seen nor perceived)
		tricks (moving table-cloth and glasses in prologue; vibrating cups in café)	
Digital post-production special effects	Morphings and warpings 3D animations and computer-generated images Some colour effects (saturation) Talking photos Acelerated/slow-motion shots Inlays (arrows, text)	Blue-screened shots to introduce several 'layers' (dreams, flashbacks) Compositing and insertion of objects, images Touched-up skies Matte paintings First stylised shot of café façade Gnome photographs	Deletion of unwanted objects in public places Colour grading process (touched-up skies)

The flexibility of digital editing

As well as special effects, some innovative digital editing applications using Duboicolor were pioneered for *Amelie*. The images were scanned and transferred to a computer for the non-linear editing:

> The arrival of digital technology, which wasn't around for *Delicatessen*, has changed everything substantially. For *City Of Lost Children*, we were able to do all of the special effects in digital. Now, with Amelie, we did the cutting in digital. We didn't cut the negative. I think we're entering a new period of filmmaking that's analogous to switching from black-and-white to colour, or from silent to sound. The medium is completely flexible now, and it's not bound by anything. If you imagine something, you can do it.[38]

Non-linear digital editing extends the possibilities of image composition and facilitates the insertion of special effects. Speed of movement can be manipulated, introducing slow motion to create the surreal atmosphere of the ghost train for example. Conversely, accelerated shots simulate a compression of time and provide light comedy effects. They also dramatise the narrative, by adding pace and stylisation to the construction of the concierge's love letter for example, or by enhancing the feeling of exhilaration when Nino and Amélie ride around Paris.

These strategies are combined with more traditional editing and punctuation marks: a split screen combines two simultaneous spaces (the light signals at the window in two parts of Paris); a horizontal wipe suggests the passage of time (teddy bear in the snow); a vertical wipe marks an elliptical change of space from the station to the café (when Amélie arrives at her father's, and for the visit to Collignon's parents); and fade to white is used as a punctuation mark to close certain sequences, for example when Amélie, and then Nino, discover the identity of the photo-booth stranger. These devices serve different purposes in turn dramatic or aesthetic, and contribute to the poetic and dreamy atmosphere of the film.

Beyond generating spectacle and fantasy, the numerous manipulations and special effects mentioned in this section affect the authenticity and realism of the film. In some cases they can compromise the reliability of the filmed image. For instance, viewers may start wondering which shots are touched up, and which vintage video footage really is taken from authentic television programmes, or whether it was re-created and aged artificially for the occasion, just like the concierge's letter in the story. However, as many visual effects are designed to be imperceptible, they become difficult to trace. The audience would not be aware of the majority of the subtle aesthetic corrections and playful details added in postproduction, were it not for interviews and DVD commentary.

The use of sound

Amelie's visual style may well have attracted most of the critical attention, but the soundtrack constitutes another crucial element of the success of the film. If Yann Tiersen's waltz, which serves as theme to the film, has now become world-famous, other sound elements beyond the musical score also contribute to its identity, including dialogue, inventive sound effects and the role of the voiceover narrator.

Figure 5: Digital editing: constructing Madeleine Wallace's letter.

Dialogue, wit and Mots d'Auteur

As suggested in Chapter Two, communication is not the forte of most of the characters in *Amelie*. The main protagonist was never offered the chance to express herself as a child, and her attempts to start a conversation with her taciturn father when she has something on her mind are doomed, as this short dialogue illustrates:

(Father is cleaning the gnome.)

(Amélie)   – *Dad, if you found a precious relic from your childhood, how would it make you feel? Happy? Sad? Nostalgic? What?*
(Father)   – *I did not have the gnome when I was a child […]*
(Amélie)   – *No. I mean something you hid like a secret treasure…*
(Father)   – *I should varnish him before the autumn.*

As a result, Amélie often prefers not to intervene in conversations unless absolutely necessary. She often observes and listens passively, as her visits to the concierge's lodge, and to Collignon's parents, illustrate. More importantly, she seems to lose all her communication skills in key moments, as when she meets Bretodeau in a café, and Nino at *Les Deux Moulins*. Conversely, Lucien's emancipation from Collignon's overbearing attitude passes by a verbal flow of humorous rhyming insults, 'Collignon tête à gnons' (big moron). In both cases, Dufayel, the painter, acts as a mediator, with whom both Amélie and Lucien can open up and express themselves more freely.

Humour often characterises the dialogue. For example, it is conveyed through Lucien and Amélie's obsession with 'Lady Di' – he wants to see a star named after her, she uses the pretext of a petition to canonise Lady Di when she calls on the various 'Bredoteaus' listed in the directory. The dialogue also brings secondary characters to life, as shown by Georgette's distinctive accent or Lucien's childish delivery. In this respect, it is typical that Gina should assess Nino's character by asking him to quote the endings of traditional proverbs,

Figure 6: The travelling gnome.

arguing that 'someone who knows his proverbs can't be all bad'. In addition, the film contains numerous *mots d'auteur* in the form of rhyming couplets, puns, aphorisms and witty lines such as the street prompter's cue 'at least, you'll never be a vegetable as even artichokes have hearts'. They are often untranslatable but have significantly contributed to the success of the film in France.

The dialogue of *Amelie* is self-conscious, but it is designed to produce precise effects and trigger memories. It places the film within the tradition of popular French screenwriting, often associated with Poetic Realism,[39] and also with more recent trends such as the *policier* films written by Michel Audiard, or the comedies of the Splendid group. This gives the screenplay its popular quality, through a series of fragments of simple, matter-of-fact conversations reflecting the characters' lives and preoccupations. Yet *Amelie*'s dialogue can intrigue viewers, especially foreign ones, as it has little in common with their experience of more introspective social realism, or the intellectual less accessible wordiness associated with the French '*auteur*' films of the 1990s. A typical example of this is the use made of the omniscient narrator.

The role of the narrator

The role assigned to the narrator (André Dussollier) is significant and original. Although never visible, his presence in voiceover mode is explicitly felt from the first shot, highlighting his omniscient status. His first function is to explain Amélie's personality by providing an insight into her unusual childhood. In the way of an authoritative documentary voiceover, he informs the spectator of her emotions and thoughts – thus complementing the information provided by the plot and images.

However, the narrator in *Amelie* is not entirely reliable, and his interpretation of facts can be questioned. He acts as both conscience and commentator, providing factual but also subjective information. Unlike the supposedly impartial narrator of a documentary, he seems to have a vested interest in the well-being and happiness of the character. His clockwork precision, sense of detail and knowledge of the future may be seen as excessively domineering, hence suspect. On the one hand, he acts as a guardian angel or benevolent 'God figure' following his protégée, on the other hand, the trivial but seemingly scientific information that he provides seems to bring together unconnected random events emphasising contingency and placing Amélie's life within a chaotic universe.[40]

In many respects, the voiceover brings in an element of subjectivity, which could be assimilated to the voice of the director himself, who openly admits his desire to control everything. The constant interventions of the narrator can be compared to Jeunet's own filming method, and read as a metaphorical inscription of authorial discourse within the film, imposing authority over the story. They also function as a cohesive device within the narrative, as does the musical score written by Yann Tiersen.

Accordion and waltz in Montmartre: Yann Tiersen's score

Undoubtedly, music is a crucial component of *Amelie*'s mood, and a key element of its popular success. And yet, Yann Tiersen was chosen in circumstances not dissimilar to the chance events that punctuate the film. Jeunet heard a Tiersen album (*Le Phare/The Lighthouse*, 1998) in a friend's car, liked it and, as a result, approached the musician. He selected several existing tracks and tested them against the images of the film before commissioning Tiersen to write the remainder.[41] Ten out of 18 tracks of the *Amelie* album were composed in 2001, including the main theme 'La Valse d'Amélie'. Tiersen read the screenplay but did not see the film before he composed these tracks. In any case, he claims that he cannot write music to illustrate images. This approach fitted in well with Jeunet's working method, as it allowed him to pick and choose the extracts that he wanted more freely.

Tiersen occupies a special place on the French musical scene.[42] Formally trained at the *Conservatoire*, he is a multi-instrument artist who began composing in the 1990s, after moving away from his classical training to become involved with the rock scene (influenced by post-punk bands). His debut instrumental album *La Valse des monstres/The Monsters' Waltz* was released in 1995, followed by *Rue des cascades/ Waterfalls Road* in 1996. Both provided several pieces for the *Amelie* soundtrack, for instance, 'La Valse des monstres' is played as Amélie re-creates Madeleine Wallace's letter. Although these two albums were little noticed by the critics or the public, they contributed to Tiersen being increasingly present at festivals and on regional stages – in particular in his native Brittany, where he made a name for himself thanks to his innovative and versatile stage performances. In 1998, his third album *Le Phare* reached a wider audience before providing another three tracks for the film, as did 'Tout est calme' in 1999. Tiersen also composed music for short films and plays, and contributed to various film soundtracks. For instance 'La rupture' appears in *Alice et Martin* (André Téchiné, 1998), and 'Rue des cascades' is the theme tune of *La Vie rêvée des anges/Dreamlife of Angels* (Erick Zonca, 1998).

Sometimes compared to Michael Nyman and Pascal Comelade,[43] Tiersen has developed a style that draws its inspiration from various popular and classical sources. Like many artists of his generation, he uses traditional instruments such as the mandolin, the guitar and especially the accordion, which contribute to the retro sound of his music, but also, as Phil Powrie has pointed out, as a marker of community often associated with Paris in cinema.[44] Tiersen's music has a timeless quality that matches *Amelie*'s mood and its romantic love motif. In addition the soundtrack reinforces the nostalgic atmosphere that characterises the film. Making extensive use of the accordion and of waltz tempos, it is delicate and emotional, but also repetitive, obsessive and intriguing. Used as the central theme, 'La Valse d'Amélie' is deployed in different instrumental versions, echoing the motif of the merry-go-round, but also evoking a bitter-sweet melancholy. It recalls the French popular tradition of accordion music of the 1930s and 1950s, but it also signals the renewed interest in acoustic music at the end of the 1990s exemplified in France by young artists such as San Severino or Mano Solo. Music in *Amelie* fulfils several functions. On the one hand, as a non-around complement to the narrative, it echoes in turn Amélie's happiness, her emotions and her mobility as she travels round Paris. On the other hand, two 1930s classic songs are integrated diegetically into the film. The jazzy 'Guilty' (1931) is heard as background music in the café scenes, and Fréhel's 'Si tu n'étais pas là' (1934) is played on the blind man's old gramophone in the metro scene, retaining the authentic crackling sounds associated with old records.

Both self-consciously nostalgic and contemporary, Tiersen's soundtrack thus falls into the category of 'postmodern' music, thus complementing the visual features of the film. It also reinforces the retro mood of the film and, more specifically, a sense of loss and the nostalgia for bygone times. This is highlighted by the motifs of absence and loss that are central to the narrative of the film and to Tiersen's music. Released in 2001 the album *L'Absente/The Absent Woman* provided two pieces for the soundtrack of *Amelie*. However, unlike Jeunet, who puts forward his nostalgic fascination for the past, Tiersen tends to reject the nostalgia associated with his music, on the ground that he does not feel drawn towards the past, but rather looks towards the future. One element that links Tiersen to Jeunet's world, though, is the fact that he composes music to 'channel emotions, pin down moments and create his own landmarks'.[45]

The 'retro minimalism' of Tiersen's music may initially appear to contradict the fascination with new technologies that characterises *Amelie*. However, Tiersen recycles retro rhythms and melodies such as the waltz and the foxtrot, experimenting with them and creating his own arrangements. In this respect, his creative process is comparable with Jeunet's, whose cinematic style relies on recycling retro atmospheres digitally to create a personal world that, as Powrie argues, is made of 'nostalgic retrospection' and uses pre-existing recycled music.[46] Both the musician and the director resort to 'bricolage', which is essentially a postmodern form of creation.

Tiersen's music is perceived as unusual because it departs in an original way from the mainstream rhythms of pop music and 'easy listening'. In the 1990s, he was linked with 'alternative' musical circles, which promoted a craftsman-like eclectic conception of music as culturally authentic, especially in their stage performances. This movement has increasingly been main-streamed due to the success and institutionalisation of the java/waltz motif in recent forms of French *chanson*.[47] Yet, Tiersen's music is also conservative because it re-appropriates the ethnocentric conventions of the nation's past, in a way that is not dissimilar to the integration of blues or reggae within American culture. This mixture of originality and conservatism identified in Tiersen's music also largely applies to *Amelie*, just as his trajectory from alternative to mainstream music echoes Jeunet's evolution from *Delicatessen* to *Amelie*. For all these reasons, what started with the chance meeting of a film-maker and a musician who construct distinctive worlds of their own turned into the effective fusion of two modes of artistic expression to produce *Amelie*.

A profusion of sound effects

As ambient sound conditions the mood and rhythm of *Amelie*, it is worth considering how other forms of non-verbal, non-musical sound effects are used in the film. Diegetic background noises, such as a steaming coffee machine in the café, ringing telephones and funfair music, punctuate the film. Some of these sounds illustrate an image, such as the exaggerated effect of the movement of the clock hand for example. Other sounds come from off-screen sources, which implies that viewers are left to imagine the source. These include church bells (of Sacré-Coeur?), trains in the distance, and other noises which evoke a village-like atmosphere. For example, for a fraction of a second, a crow is heard when Amélie is at the grocer's. Interestingly, these sounds, which (wrongly?) suggest spontaneity and randomness, tend to contradict the artificial manipulation of the images to achieve specific effects. In fact, the DVD commentary tends to confirm that they are mostly consciously added in post-synchronisation.

Non-diegetic sounds are assigned other functions. They highlight the playfulness of the film and its collage structure, as the example of the concierge's letters illustrates. As Amélie reads them, a male voice is introduced into the *mise-en-scène* and a number of sound illustrations can be heard in the background, evoking the places where they were written: we hear in turn a train, church bells and a military clarion. Later, when the concierge reads the letter recomposed by Amélie, fragments borrowed from the original letters resurface, including the sounds that accompanied specific sentences. A playful Jeunet takes the pastiche and collage activities to extremes of precision and sense of detail. The letter is fake but its fragments appear to be authentically reproduced, even though the DVD commentary suggests that they do not strictly match.

Only about five per cent of *Amelie*'s sound was post-synchronised. Some non-diegetic sounds and sound special effects were added at the editing stage to reinforce the continuity of the action. These often act as punctuation in the film grammar, marking the opening or the end of a scene. As Dudley Andrew puts it, 'Most of *Amelie*'s shots are marked with distinct beginnings and ending points to allow neighboring shots to couple in a train of micro-occurrences. The soundtrack emphasises this tactic, as virtually every scene and many individual shots conclude with audible finality.'[48] These include diegetic sounds such as trains and birds, as well as noises and cartoon-like mimetic sounds. Characteristically, the non-diegetic music does not always stop when a scene ends, it overlaps into the next scene smoothing the transition process and acting as a cohesive device.

There are times in the film when sound effects become fully integrated into the narrative, clarifying the action. For example when Collignon's feet do not fit into his slippers because Amélie has swapped them for a smaller size, it is through sound effects that his dismay is expressed. Similarly, at the end of the film, when Amélie imagines her future with Nino, daydream and reality merge with the muffled sound of the bead curtain in the kitchen. This is immediately followed by the rational explanation of the cat's meow. In this case, the aural effect precedes the image. In a more traditional way, some sounds reinforce a climactic moment in the narrative. Amélie's discovery of the box in the wall recess is dramatised by a loud 'whooshing' sound, while the theme music serves to highlight the character's emotion and excitement. More cartoon-like whooshing sounds are introduced into the soundtrack, suggesting movement and speeding up the narrative. These emphasise Amélie's spatial mobility, and serve to establish transitions between scenes, or to signal a change of location.

The role assigned to sounds and music in *Amelie* extends far beyond the merely decorative. An important element of the *mise-en-scène* and narrative stategies, the soundtrack fully contributes to the construction of the distinctive atmosphere associated with the film. As a synthetic conclusion, the close study that follows illustrates how the various sound and visual properties discussed above combine to form a typical sequence of *Amelie*.

The blind man scene

The 'blind man scene' brings together the motif of solidarity and dazzling use of cinematography. It starts with a happy Amélie walking in Paris, having anonymously returned the box of toys to Bretodeau and witnessed the consequences of her scheme. As the narrator informs us, this fills her with 'a strange feeling of absolute harmony' and 'an urge to help mankind'. The first opportunity appears in the form of a blind man who needs help to cross the street and make his way to the metro.

This sequence shows how the loosely constructed plot allows for digressions to punctuate the narrative to underline the sense of local space and community. In this case its function is to offer a visual feast anchored in everyday life. The initial shots highlight the stylisation of the city, although the scene is filmed on location and based on a form of reality. On the Pont des Arts, soft lighting is used, suggesting that Amélie is in harmony with the city. A tracking Steadycam camera moves around her as she walks over. Its fluid movement together with the use of slow motion emphasise her light-hearted mood and communicative happiness. This contrasts with the change of pace, marked by brisk editing and increasingly frantic camera movements as the scene progresses towards its climax.

The blind man is introduced in two stages, repeating a strategy already used for Nino and Amélie. The camera is initially placed near the ground, showing his feet, the white stick and the kerb before moving up to his face. A spectacular zoom forward on Amélie is meant to capture her point of view and intention to help the blind man. The express tour of the street is marked by fast cutting and rapid changes in the focus of attention, which literally take the viewers for a ride, influencing or confusing their viewing experience. For 30 seconds, they are transported into another world, just as the blind man becomes a part of the world of those who can see. The scene ends on a spectacular effect. A flash of light coming from the sky literally envelops the blind man, visually illustrating the warmth that he felt for a few seconds, by being included into the lives and small pleasures of ordinary people that he cannot see.

The effectiveness of the scene owes a lot to the soundtrack which combines verbal elements, diegetic sounds evoking a buzzing local community, non-diegetic music and sound effects added in postproduction. Amélie's comments bring a synaesthetic charm to the scene, associating traditional food with colours, odours and flavours (melons, roast chicken, lollipops and ice cream). In the first part, the familiar accordion theme associated with Amélie and Paris serves as a form of narrative punctuation, used whenever she has successfully performed a good deed. Further on, the fast rhythm of the track 'La Noyée' lends itself well to the frantic 'guided tour'. As for the enchanting buzzing atmosphere of the street, it is suggested by rustling sounds, bringing a magical touch to daily routine. For the first time the shy and withdrawn Amélie is able to express herself uninhibitedly, and she feels at home among the 'little people' of Paris.

Paris and its 'little people'

Paris has often been fantasised cinematically as a romantic and mysterious city, and N.T. Bihn's recent book *Paris au cinéma* refers to the Paris of *Amelie* as a fairytale city.[49] Jeunet's film joins an impressive series of classics set in Montmartre over the years: *French Cancan* (Jean Renoir, 1955), *Les 400 Coups* (François Truffaut, 1959), *Zazie dans le métro* (Louis Malle, 1960) or *Lautrec* (Roger Planchon, 1998) to name a few.[50] This fascination with Montmartre is not limited to French productions, as over the years, international cinema too has yielded to its appeal in productions as diverse as *An American in Paris* (Vincente Minnelli, 1951) and *Moulin Rouge* (Baz Luhrmann, 2001). However, Paris, in *Amelie*, is more than merely a décor, and this section examines how it is represented and what role it plays in the narrative.

It is predominantly the *Paris populaire* in the French sense of 'Paris of little people' that is being explored via Amélie's travels in and out of the city. This is nevertheless contrasted with brief, but regular incursions into the suburbs, when Amélie visits her father. Apart from short scenes at Notre-Dame, at the canal Saint-Martin, on le Pont des Arts, in la Foire du Trône, and in Bretodeau's Rue Mouffetard, *Amelie* is mainly set in the emblematic Montmartre.[51]

Montmartre and Paris's popular heritage

Rich in contrast and local colour, Montmartre is a multicultural district situated to the north of the city. Built on a hill dominating Paris (la butte), it forms the 18th Arrondissement, extending to the west towards Les Batignolles, and touching to the east the popular area of la Goutte d'Or. It is bounded in the north by the district of Clignancourt, and to the south by Pigalle from Place de Clichy to Boulevard Rochechouart. Because of their proximity, Montmartre and Pigalle are often amalgamated by tourists, and considered as the two sides of the same coin, the former known for its traditional village atmosphere and its artistic heritage, the latter for its nightlife and more sleazy reputation (strip-tease clubs, sex shops and prostitutes). In *Amelie*, we are only presented with daytime Montmartre, if we leave aside the heroine's short visit to a Boulevard de Clichy sex shop, which is clearly not part of her world.

Montmartre projects a multiple image, combining a colourful, bohemian lifestyle with an historical and artistic heritage. In the first place, it is viewed as an artists' quarter, immortalised at the end of the nineteenth century by such illustrious residents as Renoir, Toulouse-Lautrec, Poulbot, Van Gogh, Verlaine, Zola and Satie. This artistic tradition has been perpetuated in the twentieth century by major artists like Utrillo and Picasso, and to this day, Montmartre remains associated with (street) artists, galleries and studios. To some extent, Pigalle, too, retains connections with the artistic sphere with its theatres and music-hall shows. Once branded a centre of decadent entertainment with mythic cabarets, like Aristide Bruant's *Le Lapin agile*, and music halls like *Le Moulin rouge*, it has developed into a tourist red-light district and notorious centre of nightlife.

Montmartre remains a major tourist spot, with its winding cobbled streets and squares, boutiques, cafés, artist galleries, and particularly the Sacré-Coeur basilica, which dominates the city. As a result, it has a special place in the collective imagery associated with Paris, for French people as well as foreigners.[52] Having lived there since he moved to the capital in the 1970s, Jeunet's representation of Montmartre reflects his own ambivalent perception of the place, as the picturesque and magical part of the capital seen by the outsider that he once was on the one hand, and the centre of a village-like community that he has now become integrated with on the other.

Key locations of Amélie's Montmartre

Shooting *Amelie* in a busy part of Paris like Montmartre was not an easy option, especially for a first experience outside studios. Jeunet was helped by the fact that he could use colourful real locations that did not require too much additional set design. For Collignon's grocery located in a recessed angle of the Rue des Trois-Frères, the existing shop 'Au Marché de la butte' only underwent minor alterations. Linking Pigalle to the old Montmartre, the 'real' café where Amélie works, *Les Deux Moulins* in Rue Lepic stands strategically halfway between two cultural landmarks: Toulouse-Lautrec's *Moulin Rouge* and Renoir's *Le Moulin de la Galette*.

Amélie's flat is fictitiously located in a traditional Parisian building, complete with concierge and indoor courtyard at number 56 of the same Rue des Trois-Frères. The interior was re-created in studio for the shooting. Special emphasis is placed on the stairs and landings leading to the different flats, which feature in several scenes, recalling the imagery of Poetic Realism. However, in *Amelie*, these are used mostly as spaces of encounter and exchange linking the residents, and as a pretext to complex cinematography. In *Le Jour se lève*, conversely, the staircase is assigned the important dramatic function of providing the only access to the recluse hero. It links the room (prison) with the outer world, and provides a confined public space where many characters discuss and comment on events.

As transit places between Paris and the suburbs, train stations feature prominently in the film, primarily as meeting points for Amélie and Nino. Blending shots of the Gare du Nord and Gare de l'Est, which are in reality half a mile apart, the film re-creates a semi-fictional station that epitomises the semi-realist representation strategy of the film based on bricolage and hybridity. Most scenes take place inside, fully exploiting the large spaces of hallways, tracks and platforms, and the natural light effects of glass-panelled roofing and semi-circular glazed façades. The use of glass and metal structures emphasises the urban context of the film and evokes the Paris of Gustave Eiffel.

Figure 7: The Metro station Abbesses.

Chosen partly for their distinctive styles, the local metro stations too participate in the narrative. With its blue plates, tiled walls and colourful period posters, the Art Nouveau station of 'Abbesses' provides a striking setting for ordinary routine, as does the unusual entrance of 'Lamarck-Caulaincourt' set into the hillside. The open-air station of La Motte-Picquet Grenelle, where Amélie places the 'Wanted' fliers, is identified by its metallic stairs and frosted glass panels. As for the more conventional shots of the aerial metro, they symbolise Amélie's increasing mobility across the capital, as the game of hide-and-seek between her and Nino develops.

The contradictions of a stylised, timeless Montmartre

Although shot mainly on location, *Amelie* mythologises Montmartre at least as much as it captures its reality, resorting to elusive truth, selective fragmentation and cosmetic changes. In many exterior shots, the modern urban elements that do not fit in with the fairytale atmosphere of the film have been deleted. The result is an idealised representation of Montmartre as a clean, non-threatening version of Paris, a playground with funfairs and merry-go-rounds, championing a convivial village-like atmosphere.[53] Public places become potential social meeting points, and settings for adventure and romance. Safe and consensual, the Paris of *Amelie* promotes a popular narrative. As Sallie Westwood and John Williams argue in *Imagining Cities*, 'Popular narratives [...] actually *domesticate* the city, taking out the *risqué* element and making it safe.'[54] Even the indirect reference to Pigalle's nightlife is 'domesticated' in the subdued scene of the sex shop, in a conscious effort to preserve the amusingly 'cute' spirit of the film.

Many images evoke working-class, popular areas, and resuscitate a past imagery rendered familiar, for example, by the artist Robert Doisneau, a close friend of Prévert. His photographs, taken in Paris from the 1930s onward, often feature ordinary people at work or in a family context. Doisneau places the emphasis on movement and spontaneity, and captures daily routine or special moments, with optimism and humour.[55] His photographs have contributed to promote a popular image of Paris and ordinary people, and for years they have been reproduced on posters, cards and calendars, sold all over the world. *Amelie*'s imagery too tries to reproduce this ordinariness and spontaneity, in the street, in the microcosm of the café, or in the concierge's lodge with its clutter of objects from another time.

By blending shots of the present-day Montmartre with a variety of recycled past images, *Amelie* (re)constructs a timeless Paris,[56] and activates two contradictory impulses that feed the aesthetic representation of the city. On the one hand, the film is driven by a realist impulse legitimised by the authenticity of location shooting and an anchoring into daily routine. On the other hand, the locations go through a stylisation process facilitated by colour manipulation and the introduction of special effects. Temporal markers are voluntarily blurred, and as a result, the image of Montmartre presented in the film is ambivalent, bringing to mind at once an undefined past and a glossy tourist brochure. The scene with Collignon in the middle of the night, for example, features the shadow of a tall façade, which recalls the popular Paris of Poetic Realism, mythologised by (rather than filmed in) exceptional sets designed in studios.[57] Other shots perpetuate the tradition of staging the city's rooftops, angular buildings and cobbled streets.

The residents of this 'village-in-the-city' are colourful 'little people' – the regulars of a bar, the local grocer and his assistant, the concierge, the painter, but also cameo figures like the beggar who does not work on Sundays and the sex-shop assistant. They promote a popular sense of community, which is not dissimilar to that explored in another film set in Paris, *Chacun cherche son chat* (Cédric Klapisch, 1996).[58] In both cases, the plots, designed to help the two heroines in their identity quest, emphasise the relationship between space and community, as well as nostalgia for the past. The latter, however, contains an explicit denunciation of the destruction of popular Paris and the uprooting of the local population by trendy new residents, which anchors it in today's real political context. Conversely, the urban myth presented in *Amelie* is not socially grounded into the present reality (ethnic and sexual diversity, drug-dealing, etc.). It simply pays tribute to the little people of an idealised Paris.

The tension between realism and stylisation in *Amelie*'s Paris is further complicated by Jeunet's ambiguous comments: 'I tried to work outside as if I was on a stage. We modified a lot of the reality. But it was important that the film take place in the Paris of today, not in some kind of timeless dimension. For example, we changed things on the walls, got rid of graffiti, added signs.'[59] Jeunet does not acknowledge the timelessness of *Amelie*'s Paris, but confirms the 'staging' of his exterior scenes to control the filmed images to make them fit with his own idealised vision of the city. Whether intended or not, the 'modifications' that he describes in interviews do prevent a realistic representation of today's Paris, and result in a degree of stylisation.

In *Amelie*'s stylised world, time is an elusive concept. Here, Philip Drake's study of 'retro' trends in recent Hollywood cinema offers a useful point of reference. Drake argues that '[retro] film narratives can dramatise the relationship between past and present, constructing a memory of the past through the recycling of particular iconography that metonymically comes to represent it'.[60] Retro films mobilise specific codes, including the 'memorialisation' of the past and its re-imagining within the present. The essence of the retro film is timelessness, a fusion of past and present, or in Drake's words, 'a playful deployment of the past in the present'.[61] In the case of *Amelie*, this past/present ambiguity feeds the narrative. For example, Amélie's quaint world is linked to an (imagined?) past, yet it remains connected to the present reality by bringing the real-life events of 1997 into the fictional narrative. Similarly, Tiersen's soundtrack combines retro rhythms and instruments with the more modern repetition techniques of the 1990s.[62] In both cases, a fusion of past and present operates, which draws upon an undefined timelessness that appeals to the collective popular memory. It blurs the distinction between the real and the myth, the past and the present, to generate a sense of stylised *pastness*, relying upon mediated memory and selectivity, or in James Austin's words, 'a past emptied of its content but retaining the gloss of the attractive surface'.[63]

The artificial recycling of virtual past atmospheres and individual memories encourages nostalgia. Various recycling strategies are employed in *Amelie*, including pastiche, collage and quotation, to bring to life Amélie's memories of her own childhood, the concierge's past, the painter's experience and Collignon's father's youth. These point at postmodern aesthetics and encourage the eclectic creation of new out of old: the fake letter that Madeleine Wallace receives from her late husband represents a case in point. Amélie borrows the idea from a real-life event related in the newspaper about a post-bag lost in a crash in the 1950s and recovered years later. As Ginette Vincendeau noted, 'The device could stand as an image of the narrative itself, with its collage structure, sentimentality and fake ageing.'[64] Moreover, the scene is filmed using accelerated shots, which symbolically enhances the compression of time and history.

The nostalgic appropriation of Paris in *Amelie* has enchanted, concerned or angered the viewers, and become one of the most critically discussed elements of the film. However, by recycling and stimulating the collective memories fed by many past pictorial and cinematic sources, and by bringing in his own personal imagery of the city, Jeunet has successfully created an enticing postmodern cityscape, which contributed to the success of the film, and is part and parcel of his aesthetic signature.

Jeunet's postmodern signature

In some ways, *Amelie*'s postmodern quality strives to reconcile the contrasting traditions of Hollywood and French cinema. But in others, Jeunet's distinctive style dissociates him from both. If he does import into his film a number of Hollywood high-tech production values, he moves away from its practices, which limit directorial control. More importantly, although he is influenced by the legacy of Poetic Realism, he overtly dismisses that of the French New Wave. His references to Truffaut are anecdotal quotations (the fly visible on screen in *Jules et Jim*) or playful winks (the flight of pigeons), which happen to match *Amelie*'s imagery.[65]

The film's commitment to spectacular aesthetics can also be read as a reaction against the gritty realism of French cinema in the 1990s, and the critics' stigmatisation of beautiful images as suspect: 'Some people argue that the aesthetic side of a film can be at the expense of emotion, but as far as I am concerned, I cannot understand why a film should be ugly to be moving.'[66] In this, he echoes the positions of Besson, Beineix or Leconte, who have also been denigrated for producing spectacular surface effects rather than achieving the personal commentary on the world associated with *auteur* cinema. Jeunet's animation background and advertising aesthetics point at the legacy of *cinéma du look*. But *Amelie* also recalls other postmodern films of the 1990s, especially *Lola Rennt/Run, Lola Run* (Tom Tykwer, 1998), which had first experimented with distinctive *mise-en-scène* strategies found in Jeunet's film, such as the use of the clock, the role played by the city space, the fast editing and the use of black and white as a narrative device.

Amelie celebrates the triumph of imagination over realism, highlighting a number of curious analogies between Jeunet and his main character. They both exist in fantasy worlds rather than reality, preferring childish games and playful treasure hunts to more direct confrontations with the real world and the present. Both express themselves by practising collage and pastiche, recycling existing images and memories thanks to technology. Just like Amélie in the film narrative, the impulse of Jeunet's creativeness is a combination of his own imagination and his playful disposition, both being fed with memories accumulated over the years: 'My world is that of childhood and I don't try to conceal it. [...] I like the playful, Meccano box side of cinema.'[67] Striving for immediate effects often associated with immaturity and childhood, the film negotiates a balance between calculated effects and emotion, magic fantasy and controlled mechanical processes.[68] It combines the values of personal cinema with state-of-the-art digital special effects, drawing equally upon the legacy of French cinema and transnational commercial practices. These paradoxes reinforce the postmodern nature of the film, not just in its narrative and genre mixing suggested in Chapter Two, but also in its distinctive use of visual imagery and music, which were the focus of this chapter.

In addition, *Amelie* rejects the superiority of classic art over popular culture. It brings together images of all sorts and origins (posters, videos, newsreels, adverts and paintings), which are appropriated to be consumed again, initially by the characters and, by extension, the viewers (Renoir's painting, the concierge's letters). These beautiful images are primarily designed for consumption, as are the profusion of objects in Amélie's world. The film displays a fetishist fascination with collections (the photo album, the treasure box) and quaint objects, assigning to them symbolic or dramatic values. For example, the marshmallow machine in the final scene can be seen as the *mise en abyme* of Amelie's lack of ideological depth, and an overt acknowledgement by Jeunet of the playful nature of his film. This is complemented by a series of 'confectionary' metaphors used in reviews to evoke the film's 'sugariness,'[69] that is to say a colourful and sweet pleasure that melts and disappears. This tends to be contradicted by the fact that the film hit an emotional chord with many viewers and triggered an ideological debate. It confers to images (even glossy ones) the power to generate plural meanings.

While confirming the hybridity of Amelie, this chapter has revealed the coherence underpinning the film, as well as correspondences between style and narrative. For example, it has exposed analogies between the manipulative schemes of Amélie and the special effects of the film; mimetic echoes between the circularity of the narrative and the use of music; and comparable metaphors of 'bricolage' in the storyline and the film editing process. Through parody, mimetic self-deprecation, and a *mise en abyme* of the film-making process within the narrative, form and content combine to provide a comprehensive insight into Jeunet's signature. *Amelie* started as an original personal project, and became a phenomenal popular success. It is now time to consider the circumstances of its reception, without which this critical study would not be complete.

Notes

1   A. Ferenzci, '*Un long dimanche de fiançailles*', *Télérama* 2859 (27 October 2004).
2   E. Frois and J.-L.Wachthausen, 'Jeunet: j'ai le sentiment d'être mort en 14', *Figaro*, 27 October 2004.
3   J. St Clair, 'Celebrating reproduction', *Iowa Review*, 2001, Web review, http://www.uiowa. edu/~iareview/reviews/justinstclair.htm, accessed 13 December 2003.
4   Tirard: 1997, p.122.
5   A. Martin, *Once Upon a Time in America* (London: BFI, 1998), p.10.
6   Jeunet in 'Take 5: Which films inspire you more' Website, http://movies.channel.aol. com/feature/take5/jeunet.adp, accessed on 6 January 2005. See for example the scene with the blind man in the Abbesses metro station, in which the resounding music was inspired by Kubrick, according to the DVD commentary.
7   P. Rouyer and C. Vassé, 'Entretien Jean-Pierre Jeunet: dans une autre vie je suis mort à la guerre de 14', *Positif* 525 (November 2004), pp.8–12 (p.10).
8   Ferenzci: 2004.
9   See Garbarz's analysis, 'La Recolleuse de morceaux', *Positif* 483 (May 2001), pp.29–30. Cinema's relationship with painting is very present in contemporary cinema, e.g. *La belle Noiseuse* (Rivette, 1991) tackles the relationship between the artist and his model(s); in *Les Amants du pont neuf* (Carax, 1990) a visually impaired Michèle expresses herself through art.
10 Jeunet, in Pride: 2001.
11 See Frois and Wachthausen: 2004.
12 See Bruno Delbonnel's interview in D. Maillet, '*Un long dimanche de fiançailles*', *Technicien du film* 548 (October 2004), pp.34–38 (p.36).
13 Delbonnel, in Bergery, 'Cinematic Impressionism', *American Cinematographer*, December 2004, p.61.
14 Jeunet in Lavoignat: 2000, p.13.
15 Jeunet's project differs from Pitof's in *Vidocq* (2001), the first fully digital feature film, the latter relying almost exclusively on flashy stylistic achievements.
16 The special effect laboratory Duran was founded in 1983 by Pascal Herold and Bernard Maltaverne. In 1991, Duboi, a sister company specialising in cinema digital special effects and film processing, was founded. With about 50 staff, Duran-Duboi had by 2001 produced the special effects of over 300 films, pioneering digital equipment for colour grading and digital editing, 3D animations and website design. Their postproduction complex situated

near Paris contains 245 editing suites. The company experienced serious financial difficulties in 2003, which were partly overcome with their participation in high-profile projects including *Un long dimanche de fiançailles* in 2004. See E. Maillot, 'The Very Special Effects of Duran-Duboi', *Label France* 43 (April 2001), Website http://www.france. diplomatie.fr/label_france/ENGLISH/ART/duran_duboi/page.html, accessed on 7 February 2004.

17   Gilliam and Jeunet know each other. Gilliam was even asked by the US distributors of *Delicatessen* to present the film in the credits to help the marketing. Jeunet considers the main common ground to their respective films to be the fact that they invent a different world from their own. See joint interview in J.-P. Lavoignat, 'Magic circus', *Studio Magazine* 54 (October 1991), pp.83–85 and 138.

18   They are mostly borrowed from the regular Canal Plus programme 'L'Année du zapping'.

19   Bergery: 2004, pp.58–69.

20   For a discussion of Impressionist film, see I. Aitken, 'Into the realm of the wondrous: French cinematic impressionism', in *European Film Theory and Cinema* (Edinburgh: Edinburgh University Press, 2001).

21   References to Impressionist motifs and colours are even more evident in *Un long dimanche de fiançailles* (golden cornfields, les Halles, Gare d'Orsay...).

22   Machado's workshop is in Rue des Abbesses.

23   See Libiot: 2004. Examples of paintings that directly recall the colour schemes of *Amelie* can be seen on Machado's website, http://www.jmachado.com/en, last accessed on 12 November 2004.

24   For example, the staircase in Amélie's block evokes the '59, Rue de Lille' series. See S. Voiturin, 'Amélie Poulain fabuleusement sublime', *Sonovision* 451 (May 2001), pp.14–17 (p.14).

25   Delbonnel in Clanet and Deriaz: 2001, p.9.

26   F. Reumont, 'Le Destin de l'étalonnage numérique: Bruno Delbonnel, chef opérateur', *Technicien du film* 511 (May 2001), pp.25–28 (pp.26–27).

27   Delbonnel interview 'Kodak on film', website' http://www.kodak.com/US/en/motion/ forum/onFilm/delbonnelQA.shtml, accessed on 18 October 2004.

28   Jeunet, in Rouyer and Vassé: 2004, p. 11.

29   Reumont: 2001, p.26.

30   Jeunet in J. Calhoun, 'Amélie: fabricating a new French fable', *Entertainment Design*, 1 January 2002.

31   Tirard: 1997, p.124.

32   'Trucage et cinéma', in *Essais sur la signification du cinéma* 2 (Paris: Klinsieck, 1973), reproduced in R. Hamus-Vallée, *Les Effets spéciaux* (Paris: Cahiers du cinéma, 2004), pp.64–65.

33   See full credits for a precise breakdown of duties of the special effect and digital visual effect teams. See also Voiturin: 2001, pp.14–17.

34   Voiturin: 2001, p.14.

35   Private conversation with Bruno Delbonnel (June 2004).

36   A. Hémery, 'Alain Carsoux: le fabuleux destin d'Amélie Poulain', *SFX*, May–June 2001, pp.42–44.

37   Carsoux in Voiturin: 2001, p.16.

38   Jeunet in S. Tobias, 'Jean-Pierre Jeunet', *The Onion A.V. Club*, 31 October 2001, Website http://avclub.theonion.com/avclub3739/bonus feature1_3739.html, accessed on 24 September 2003. For more information on digital timing, see J. Silberg, 'The right timing', *Millimeter*, 1 November 2002.

39   See G. Vincendeau, 'The art of spectacle: the aesthetics of classical French cinema', in M. Temple and M. Witt (eds), *The French Cinema Book* (London: BFI, 2004), pp.147–148.

40   This argument was developed in W. Everett, 'Fractal films and the architecture of Complexity', *Studies in European Cinema*, 2, 3 (December 2005), pp. 159–172.

41   The music rights were bought for FF 1.35 million.

42   The biographical information is drawn from 'Yann Tiersen: Biography' (October 2002), http://:www.rfimusique.com/siteEn/biographie/biographie_6250.asp, accessed on 29

September 2004. See also P. Powrie, (2006) 'The fabulous destiny of the accordion in French cinema' *Changing Tunes: The Use of Pre-existing Music in Film*, P. Powrie and R.Stilwell (eds), (Aldershot: Ashgate, 2006) pp. 137–151.

43   M.-H. Martin, 'Tiersen gagnant', *Nouvel Observateur* 1798 (22 April 1999).

44   Powrie: 2006, p. 137.

45   P. Brambilla, 'Yann Tiersen, le Breton qui suit sa vague', *Construire* 23 (4 June 2002), world Wide Web http://www.construire.ch/SOMMAIRE/0223/23extra4.html, accessed on 29 September 2003.

46   Powrie: 2006, p.147.

47   In France *chanson* is distinguished from other music, as a type of music that promotes lyrics and a message. For more information and a reflection on retro trends and hybridity in recent French music, see D. Looseley, *Popular Music in Contemporary France* (London: Berg, 2003), especially pp.48–49.

48   Andrew: 2004, p.41.

49   N.T. Bihn with F. Garbarz, *Paris au cinéma: La vie rêvée de la capitale de Méliès à Amélie Poulain* (Paris: Parigramme, 2003), pp.203, 215; V. Descure and C. Casazza, *Ciné-Paris: Vingt balades sur des lieux de tournages mythiques* (Paris: Hors Collection, 2003).

50   Other films are located in different districts, for example *Sous les toits de Paris* (René Clair, 1930), *Hotel du Nord* (Marcel Carné, 1938), *Les Amants du Pont-Neuf* (Leos Carax, 1991) and *Chacun cherche son chat* (Cédric Klapisch, 1996).

51   For more information on Montmartre, see L. Chevalier, *Montmartre du plaisir et du crime* (Paris: Payot, 1995).

52   See G. Weisberg, *Montmartre and the Making of Mass Culture* (New Brunswick, NJ: Rutgers University Press, 2001), pp.1–3.

53   Vincendeau: 2001, p.25. See also Moine: 2004, p.155.

54   S. Westwood and J. Williams (eds), *Imagining Cities: Scripts, Signs, Memories* (London: Routledge, 1997), p.11.

55   See, for example, the caretaker's lodge, the shop windows...

56   For example, E. Ezra talks of a 'timeless décor', emphasising the role of attractions and funfairs that she reads as 'an invocation of another temporality, one that appears to privilege contingency over predictability'. 'The death of an icon', *French Cultural Studies* 13: 3 (October 2004), p.302.

57   Andrew: 2004, p.41. Even *Pépé le Moko* (Duvivier, 1937), mostly set in Algiers, evokes the nostalgia for the popular Paris of Place Blanche, and the music hall tradition with the singing character of Tania, interpreted by the same Fréhel who features in *Amelie*'s soundtrack.

58   In this film, the main protagonist, Chloë, another single young woman, discovers the colourful members of her local community while looking for her lost cat in the streets of the 11th Arrondissement.

59   Jeunet in Pride: 2001, pp.52–55.

60   P. Drake, 'Mortgaged to music: New retro movies in the 1990s Hollywood cinema', in P. Grainge (ed.), *Memory and Popular Film* (Manchester: Manchester University Press, 2003), pp.183–201 (p.183).

61   Drake: 2003, p.189. See also Friedberg: 1994, p.3.

62   For P. Powrie, the visual effects in *Amelie* 'immobilise the past as a present-past', and Tiersen's music 'mobilises and emotionalises the past in an affectively-charged past-present' (2006 p.150.).

63   Austin: 2004, pp. 281–299 (p.290). Pastness was used in the context of nostalgia by Jameson in *Postmodernism, or, the Cultural Logic of Late Capitalism* (Durham, NC: Duke UP, 1991).

64   Vincendeau: 2001, p.24.

65   See D. Andrew's analysis of *Amelie* in relation to the New Wave. Although he initially links the outdoor shooting in *Amelie* to *Les 400 Coups*, he argues that Truffaut or Bazin would have hated the film for reasons ranging from excessive closure, intricate editing, showy style to a lack of authenticity (2004, pp.35–37).

66   Frois and Wachthausen: 2004.

67   Frois and Wachthausen: 2004.

68   Andrew: 2004, p.38. See also Moore (2006) for a detailed analysis of the role played by technology and the mechanistic view of the world painted in *Amelie* (pp.9–19).

69   See S. Johnston, 'Jeunet's light touch casts a spell', *Screen International*, 11 May 2001, p.23. See also references to 'choux pastry' in P. Preston, 'Soft choux shuffle', *Guardian*, 7 October 2001, and 'candy coated' in R. Kempley, 'Amile: candy-coated, magically delicious', *Washington Post*, 9 November 2001.

4 From surprise hit to social phenomenon: the reception of *Amelie*

'A miracle like this will not happen to me again in a hurry' Jean-Pierre Jeunet[1]

With over 30 million cinema tickets sold worldwide and box office returns over $130 million,[2] *Amelie* was a huge commercial success. Its enthusiastic critical and public reception in France and around the world turned it into a phenomenon and a symbol of the vitality of French cinema. Surprisingly, the film, which at first seemed consensual, also generated political reaction and critical debate.

Marketing and national box office

The distribution of *Amelie* in France formed part of a carefully planned marketing strategy costing a substantial FF 11 million. Largely inspired by Jeunet's American experience, the campaign relied more on Hollywood-style test screenings and focus-group feedback than on conventional press previews, recently accused by some French directors of systematically generating unfair negative reviews before a film is given a chance of finding its audience.[3]

As was the case for Jeunet's other films, a selection of short teasers were designed, using key shots edited in flash mode to offer dramatised tasters to the film. These introduced every character emphasising their relation to Amélie and the fact that she would change their lives. The traditional trailer to the film, a concentrated feast of images and sounds, tended to bring these together to introduce *Amelie*'s surreal world in a more narrative fashion, assisted by a voiceover commentary. It used the director's reputation as a selling point, but more importantly, it overtly advertised the *Amelie* 'product' to prospective viewers as a film and a character that would change THEIR lives.

In the weeks preceding the release of the film in France, Audrey Tautou's expressive face appeared on the now cult poster in all the usual public places.

Chosen from a series designed by Laurent Luffroy available on the DVD, the selected poster featured a close-up of the fairy-like Amélie, enhanced by a contrast of green and red, the emblematic colours of the film. This poster stands out as the obvious choice, effectively translating the combination of simplicity and modern look of the film better than the more contrived composite shot featuring the café, the animal-shaped clouds or the framed photographs used in the other drafts. Amélie's face remains the image associated most readily with the film, and was retained for the DVD jackets.

As has become increasingly normal in France, a careful campaign was conducted via the French media – press, radio and television. More original was the initiative taken when the film was released: the metro station 'Abbesses' was renamed 'Station Amélie' for one day, and a free photo booth was installed. UGC cinemas, the distributors, held an 'Amélie of the month' photo competition to promote its monthly passes, then published the pictures of the winners in the UGC magazine Le Spectateur.[4] Although, traditionally, there has been some hostility in France towards such marketing strategies associated with Hollywood, the promotion of French films has evolved since 2001, increasingly adopting such practices, as the high-profile release of Huit Femmes/8 Women (François Ozon, 2002) illustrates.[5]

Although Harry Potter and the Philosopher's Stone eventually gained first place at the box office in 2001, Amelie became the most successful French film of the year with 8.85 million viewers, which translates to receipts of approximately $42 million for France alone.[6] On the first day 125,000 people saw the film, 1.2 million in the first week on 432 screens, and the number of viewers continued to increase in the second week,[7] thanks to an additional 110 prints. The film needed between 1.5 and 2 million viewers in France to recover its cost, which took less than two weeks. It then remained in the top ten of the French box office for 22 weeks. The publicity around the film, together with favourable word of mouth, had brought together audiences from all age groups and social backgrounds, Parisians and provincials.

Media discourse and critical debates

Despite their cult status, the films of Jeunet and Caro had been largely neglected by critics and academics. In France, little critical analysis of their cinema has been published to our knowledge, if we leave aside dossiers compiled by popular film magazines like Studio Magazine, which followed their career from the beginning. More surprisingly, Jeunet and Caro were also largely overlooked by Anglo-American scholars, despite the growing interest in popular cinema.[8] Guy Austin's Contemporary French Cinema seems to be the only study published in the 1990s that devoted a few pages to a reading of Delicatessen in the context of fantasy film and cinéma du look.[9] The commercial success of *Amelie* has led to a number of academic articles, which have been referenced throughout this book.

To return to the critical reception in France, *Amelie* attracted significant media interest and peripheral writing around the time of its release. It was reviewed in nearly every French newspaper and magazine, complemented by numerous interviews with the director and the main actress. A quick survey covering influential film-reviewing publications reveals that a considerable number of articles were devoted to *Amelie* in 2001–2002, including at least six in *Le Monde*, 12 in *Libération* and four in *Télérama*. This is all the more surprising since these normally show little interest in mainstream films.

The majority of articles appeared between the end of April and June, though several successive waves of interest can be identified. A few articles covered the production stage, suggesting that Jeunet's first post-Hollywood film was eagerly anticipated,[10] but the main wave of reviews appeared in April 2001, coinciding with its French release. As Jeunet likes to stress, these reviews were overwhelmingly positive, ranging from unequivocally enthusiastic to more balanced opinions listing the film's strengths with the occasional reservation. Placing *Amelie* in the context of Jeunet's career, most reviews commented on the feel-good narrative, the evocative retro atmosphere, the inventive visual style and fantasy, with a special mention for the actress's performance.[11]

A few reviews were strangely non-committal: the authors recognised the film-maker's talent in creating a distinctive world, but Thomas Sotinel started his review in *Le Monde* by emphasising the impression of being 'trapped' by the film, while in *Libération*, Didier Péron and Jean-Marc Lalanne used the term 'confinement' on several occasions.[12] Apart from Serge Kaganski's article, only a handful of articles were decidedly negative, for example the reviews of Michel Boujut in *Charlie Hebdo* and Vincent Ostria in *L'Humanité*, or François Gorin's counterpoint to Jean-Claude Loiseau's positive review in *Télérama*.[13]

A second wave of feature articles appeared throughout May and June, trying to explain the atypical success of the film,[14] and commenting on the various debates and controversies that it generated, which are discussed below. More French articles were published at the end of 2001 and into the New Year as part of the usual retrospective tributes.[15] In *Le Monde*, Jean-Michel Frodon reassessed the success of the film, attributing it to a combination of aesthetic and commercial elements, which could be summarised in a three-point 'recipe' made of fragmented narrative, naive tone and effective marketing.[16] Although he sets out to account for the different facets of the *Amelie* phenomenon, Frodon starts by referring to the film as the 'most competitive product of the year'. Not only does this question implicitly the artistic merit of the film, but it is typical of the condescending attitude of many French critics towards a popular success. Interest was revived once more at the time of the Oscar

Ceremony in 2002, prolonging the career of the film. Thus, for almost a year, a plethora of discourses and interpretations around *Amelie* could be found in the French media, in an attempt to explain its trajectory from commercial success to wide-ranging phenomenon.

Amelie, *'phénomène de société'*

The French media discourse around *Amelie* reflected the enthusiasm that it generated in viewers and reviewers alike.[17] As a popular film, *Amelie* could be watched and appreciated at different levels, as a visual feast, as a feel-good film about happiness, or as a nostalgic journey to a mythologised France. Within a few weeks, the surprise hit changed into a 'phénomène de société', a social and cultural phenomenon.[18] The film became a talking point, perceived as capturing the French 'air du temps', while providing a reliable barometer of the general mood of the nation. It produced an array of reactions of excitement, identification and rejection that extended beyond the cinematic sphere. The film's locations became tourist hot spots, property prices soared in Montmartre, and numerous stories started circulating about acts of solidarity inspired by the iconic Amélie Poulain.

Sensing that this '*Amelie* effect' could assist the presidential electoral campaign, the French political sphere suddenly showed an open interest in the film. In May, President Chirac organised a much-publicised private screening at the Elysée Palace, inviting Jeunet and his team. Prime Minister Lionel Jospin showed the film to his Cabinet, as though this could help his ministers to gain a better understanding of the 'real' France.[19] Assisted by the national media, party leaders tried to appropriate the film's values to promote their own political platforms. For example, when *Libération* undertook to ask politicians to comment upon the reasons behind the success of the film, François Bayrou, the leader of centre-right party UDF, singled out the humanist values promoted by the film, only to link them to his own political programme:

> This film belongs to a genre which used to be called fairytale, namely a world in which the wonderful prevailed. Its success shows that there is a clear demand in our societies for real humanity [...] that is denigrated by intellectuals, but felt by all of us in our lives. It was in this spirit that I called my political programme '*Human France*'. The success of the film proves that there is real demand for simple happiness and humanist values.[20]

Such a response to the film may surprise on more than one count. While Jeunet himself accepts that 'we live in a time when there are no fundamental ideals, political or other',[21] it is odd that *Amelie* should epitomise the spirit of a political programme. After all, the film was appreciated by viewers primarily for its stylised look and its simplified, idealised vision of the world, rather than as a political manifesto. Any political appropriation of the film appears suspect, considering its reassuring consensual tone and the 'absence of overt ideological discourse' discussed by a number of commentators, including Ginette Vincendeau:

> In a France where the continued unfurling of state and municipal sleaze [...] alongside revelations about the country's inglorious past [...] show politicians and political ideals to be deeply compromised, *Amélie Poulain* – which offers a national vision both totally imaginary and yet utterly recognisable – is the perfect escapist product.[22]

If *Amelie* is an 'escapist product', what conclusions can we draw from the fact that political leaders, whether left wing or right wing, should compare the film to their own vision for the future of France, thereby blurring the differences between fantasy and the real world? Either these are Utopians who promote an idealist discourse that they cannot implement, or they willingly turn their backs on the real world and attempt to sway the electorate with a consensual and retrograde discourse of reassurance. In any case, they carefully avoid any serious ideological debate, unlike some film critics, such as Jean-Michel Frodon, who, in addition to the reservations mentioned above, found particularly problematic the fact that the French public should be so receptive to *Amelie*'s retro representation of France: 'A nation that accepts – and even welcomes – a tourist-brochure representation of its own past raises a number of questions regarding its relation to the world and to the future.'[23]

However, as we saw in Chapter Three, the 'past' in *Amelie* is suggested artificially rather than re-created, and it is the result of an aesthetic project driven by fantasy. If it is undeniable that the film was given a political dimension mainly in the media, the debate seems to have been blown out of proportion. *Amelie* is not an ideological manifesto, it is just a French film that overtly asserts its identity.

National identity

Amelie raised a number of questions in terms of its representation of national identity. Various attempts at defining its 'Frenchness' were made, leading to inevitable comparisons with American cinema. According to Glenn Kenny's review in the American version of *Premiere*, the film owed its success in France and elsewhere to the fact that 'it insist[ed] upon a certain ideal of what it means to be French, or more specifically Parisian'. Kenny went on to describe the cast as 'quintessentially un-American types'.[24] Similarly, *Les Cahiers du cinéma* started their review of the film by isolating the film from other recent mainstream French productions as a very French film 'devoid of any American cinema fantasy'.[25] Vincendeau went even further, seeing in the character of Amélie a metaphor for the French Republic:

> Semi-jokingly manipulating Flaubert's phrase 'Madame Bovary, c'est moi!', Jeunet declared, 'Amélie Poulain, c'est moi!' Well, 'Amélie Poulain, c'est nous,' say the French en masse, echoed by their politicians. Perhaps after Brigitte Bardot, Catherine

Deneuve and Laetitia Casta, Amélie is the new model for Marianne, the symbol of the Republic.[26]

In other words, not only was the film – and its iconic character – directly contrasted with the dominant American cultural canons, but viewers were encouraged to identity with its consensual values of happiness, altruism and solidarity, by promoting them as original and essentially French.

When Amelie was released in 2001, world cinemas were increasingly perceived to have moved beyond the restrictive framework of nation states. In France, however, many issues relating to the globalisation of culture remained central to the national debates. In this context, it is hardly surprising that Jeunet's film should come to represent a manifestation of Frenchness and a symbol of the French 'cultural exception' mentioned in Chapter One. Audiences were aware of the national identity of the film, conveyed through specific cultural references, such as the geographical setting in popular Paris and familiar vignettes of French lifestyle (cafés, concierges, markets and accordions). As we saw earlier, the French cinematic heritage was also selectively called upon by paying homage to the classics of the 1930s and the films of François Truffaut. This was complemented by references to universal cultural landmarks and tourist attractions ranging from Renoir's paintings to the Tour de France, which are identified with French culture around the world, and reinforce the Frenchness of the film. Other references were directed more specifically at French audiences: old-fashioned objects, famous brand names and television stock footage revived collective past memories and familiar images.[27] As a result, it is no longer so surprising that prominent political figures should appropriate the positive world of Amelie, and try to integrate its simple consensual message into their own discourse.

Jeunet received a prestigious national decoration ('L'Ordre national du mérite') to mark his contribution to the promotion of French cultural values all over the world.[28] Yet, his film illustrates a number of fundamental aesthetic transformations in French cinema. For instance, if the distinctive use of special effects and digital technology in Amélie, and in other films of that year like Le Pacte des loups and Vidocq, has rejuvenated the French production, it has also contributed to the Americanisation of their production. But, as James Austin has argued, while digital special effects are often associated with an Americanisation of French cinema, here they are employed 'in the service of a cultural imaginary very different from the American one'.[29] For the films mentioned above, the use of new technologies reinvented the spectacle of traditional markers of French national identity. In the case of Amelie, it was this 'fake' representation of France that triggered a critical controversy.

Critical debates: Cannes and the 'Kaganski controversy'

As part of its rising identity as a social phenomenon, Amelie was the cause of at least two polemical debates in 2001. Firstly, it was left out of the Cannes

Festival selection; secondly, it was accused of being a reactionary showcase for National Front ideology.

In February, the film was screened by the organising committee of the Cannes Festival, which would not guarantee its selection for the official competition. To be fair to the festival organisers, the film was not fully edited at the time, and there was pressure from the production to give a prompt answer. In the light of the dithyrambic reception that the film had received by early May, the committee, through its representative Thierry Frémaux, met with explicit criticism from the press and from the public, who did not understand the reasons behind this decision.[30] The committee was accused of intellectual elitism, and, when it suggested organising a special public open-air screening as part of the festival, Jeunet declined the offer.

On 31 May 2001, Serge Kaganski launched the second debate when he published a letter in the daily *Libération*, entitled 'Amélie pas jolie', in response to an article discussing the exceptional impact of the film that he had read in the same newspaper a few days before.[31] Kaganski normally writes film reviews for the trendy cultural weekly *Les Inrockuptibles*,[32] and is a regular contributor to the established cultural radio programme 'Le Masque et la plume' on the national station France Inter. He is known for his clear positioning in favour of an *auteurist* experimental cinema, and for his (often virulent) rejection of mainstream cinema. For instance, he advocates cinema 'as a tool for a better understanding of the world, the discovery of its reality and a means to experience the passing of time'[33] rather than as a form of entertainment. Kaganski had already expressed serious reservations about Jeunet and Caro's cinematic qualities in his review of *La Cité des enfants perdus*:

> What is missing in the artificial and systematic method of Jeunet and Caro, is a kind of faith, of generosity, an opening into the real and the other. […] What does the film tell us about the world in which we live, about the desires, fears and doubts of its authors, or about us? Nothing. Caro and Jeunet invent a new genre: playful autism. Here is a mechanical and technological conception of cinema.[34]

The publication of Kaganski's letter over a month after *Amelie* was released, and in a period of generalised 'Améliemania', could be compared to putting the cat among the pigeons. To summarise briefly, Kaganski's argument was articulated around three issues: the stilted aesthetic of the film, its retrograde representation of a sanitised France and the resulting effect of promoting Le Pen's National Front ideology. More specifically, Kaganski deplored the erasure of ethnicity in the film ('nettoyage'), which contradicted the sexual and cultural diversity that characterises the real-life Montmartre and Paris in general. His article thus suggested that the world of *Amelie* promoted backward-looking and conservative values. More implicitly, it hinted that it brought back memories of the 'France de Vichy' and collaboration.[35]

Although allusions had been made previously regarding *Amelie*'s unrealistic, 'virtual' Paris,[36] Kaganski's intervention was met with an avalanche of reproachful reactions from the public, as the *Libération* public forum testified.[37] There were surprisingly few formal critical responses, except for Philippe Lançon's article in *Libération*, which backed Kaganski's view, arguing that '*Amelie* is successful because it transposes Eurodisney to Montmartre: same logic, same bewitched trompe l'œil, same cardboard cut-outs, and same sadness disguised as joy'.[38] However, a number of editorials condemned Kaganski's excessive ideological outburst, as the one published on the *Ecran noir* website illustrates:

> In [Kaganski's] 'demonstration', cinema has to be 'a medium designed to get to know the world, to discover the real and to experience the passing of time'. In a nutshell cinema must be social. But let's not worry, Jean-Pierre Jeunet is totally entitled to continue to make films his way, that is 'without any connection with the real world', though Kaganski admits that he considers these as 'anti-cinema' (sic!). We touch here on another symptom of the critical microcosm, which involves the theoretical divide, taught in film courses, between Louis Lumière against Georges Méliès. One cinema is about documentary realism, the other relies on artefact, allegory and excessive fantasy. Two distinct trends, two viewpoints on the world, two ways of making films, whose limits have become increasingly blurred, as the century progressed.[39]

The polemical debate that has come to be known as the 'Kaganski controversy' may be anecdotal, but as the *Libération* forum letters and *Ecran noir* editorial point out, it provides another illustration of the long-standing divide between the public's taste and the French *auteur*-led critical establishment. It is characterised by the latter normally rejecting popular entertainment, while promoting an *auteur*-led cinema which is supposedly more in touch with real life. This manifests itself, for instance, in the discussion around Jeunet's stylised representation of Paris. *Amelie's* Paris is artificially re-created in a way that is not dissimilar to, say, Eric Rohmer's *L'Anglaise et le duc/Lady and the Duke* (2001), in which painted sets are combined with digital technology to great effect. However, the critical response is different, depending on whether the object of discussion is considered as *auteur* cinema or popular entertainment.[40]

Nevertheless, both the Cannes incident and the Kaganski debate raise questions about the independence of the critical institutions. In each case, public pressure was exerted in support of the cause for popular French cinema. First, in the Cannes affair, the public condemned the non-selection of a successful domestic film. As Olivier Séguret argued in *Libération*, this 'perniciously implied that the Cannes institution should be accountable to the French film industry, and that it should be required to support its interests'.[41] Surely, one of the functions of film festivals is to bring an audience to films that would not otherwise be widely distributed. Films like *Amelie,* which have already reached a wide audience base, do not need this showcase as desperately. In Kaganski's case, it is hard to say whether the open letter caused such a heated (over)reaction, simply because it contradicted the popular taste. Whether we agree or not with the opinions voiced is irrelevant. More interestingly, in our society, which is often considered consensual and reluctant to enter ideological debates, for once, a controversy sparked from what, after all, was only a provocative comment made by a critic known for his bias for *auteur* cinema.

The Kaganski controversy reached the Anglo-American press, but was viewed in a detached way, gently mocking the excessively politicised views of French reviewers.[42] However, *Film Comment* published a review article in translation by French critic Frédéric Bonnaud, adopting an elitist critical stance comparable to Kaganski's, and offering to the Anglophone reader a typical, if biased, intellectual commentary on the affair.[43]

Jeunet's reaction to the polemic was rather subdued. Stressing that his film was never meant to represent Paris realistically, and that commercial success was always viewed suspiciously in France, he deplored the insulting tone of the article but did not enter the political debate directly.[44] The incident certainly did not improve his relationship with some French critics, and led to his banning *Les Inrockuptibles* from attending the press screenings of his next film. Kaganski and the media thus contributed to the continued life of *Amelie*, as did the political appropriation of the film bringing to the world's attention the potential dangers of consensus and universality.

Amelie versus 'Loft Story'

There is another way in which *Amelie* was appropriated for an ideological end. In the media, the film soon came to symbolise the resistance to the growing pressures and threats of reality television through the national cinema. As early as May 2001, the simultaneous successes of *Amelie* and of the first season of the reality show *Loft Story* (the French *Big Brother*) on commercial channel M6 led to comparative analyses in the French press, in an attempt to explain the huge public interest that both had generated, turning them into social phenomena that mirrored the changes and preoccupations of the French society of the new millennium. *Marianne* entitled its special dossier 'La France d'Amélie Poulain contre la France de Loft Story',[45] and this comparison was echoed by *Libération*, *Positif* and *Télérama*. Amélie was deemed by Jean-Michel Helvig to be 'l'anti-Loana' (the opposite of Loana, the winner of the first season of *Loft Story*), and Vincent Remy noted that there was a mirror effect between *Amelie*'s idealised world and the 'derealised' loft.[46]

What particularly struck sociologists and journalists alike was the enthusiasm shown by young audiences for both forms of spectacle. Clearly promoting a non-sexual image, Amélie had become an icon of innocent and romantic love within weeks, while on the other hand, Loana's sexual affair in front of the cameras in the Loft's swimming pool made the front page and was commented upon for weeks.[47] Paradoxically, the protagonist of a supposedly hyper-real film was perceived as more genuine than the real 'character' of the real-life show, who turned out to be rather fake.[48] This association of *Amelie* and *Loft Story* cannot be solely attributed to their taking France by storm in the same week of 2001. The media clearly took sides and expressed value judgements involving alleged good taste and bad taste and reflecting their positioning in the media realm.

International reception

According to the producer Claudie Ossard, *Amelie* had been pre-sold for FF 32 million to numerous countries by May 2001, after viewing only the script and a four-minute sample reel.[49] Following its success in France and substantial publicity budgets for its marketing abroad, the film garnered 2.15 million viewers in Germany, 1.4 million in Italy, 435,000 in Spain and 132,000 in Poland. It was a record success in Japan with 40,000 viewers in the first three weeks and 550,000 by March 2002, though it had yet to be released in the provinces.[50]

In Britain, *Amelie* was released on 5 October 2001 with a 15 certificate. Launched with a substantial £600,000 promotional campaign using the prestigious sponsor Cognac Martel, it set box-office records for a French production on its first weekend, starting with $823,000 takings and 82 prints. Another 27 prints were added a few weeks later, and uncharacteristically, the film was not restricted to art-house cinemas but was also screened in multiplexes, possibly because the UGC group runs a number of these in Britain. At the time of writing, *Amelie* remains the most successful French film in the UK with just over one million viewers (£4.32 m),[51] and a fifth place at the box office. This success is all the more significant because the film was released in French with subtitles.

Even more surprising was the way in which *Amelie* took America by storm, grossing $33.2 m.[52] The film was distributed by Miramax, a group specialising in high-profile foreign films with invaluable experience in marketing these on the limited American market. After buying the rights for $1m on its presentation at the Los Angeles market, Miramax pinned their hopes at an early stage on *Amelie*'s nomination for the 2002 Oscars, hoping to repeat the success story of *La Vita è bella/Life is beautiful* (Roberto Benigni) in 1998.[53] They launched a comparable marketing campaign, distributing it initially via the art-house circuit, with three screens in New York and Los Angeles, before extending it to 60 screens in the second week, and eventually reaching a peak of 335 prints nationwide.[54]

Articles on the film had started to appear in the British and American press as soon as the film was released in France. As early as 30 April 2001, *Variety* had reviewed the film as 'a fresh, funny, exquisitely bittersweet tour de force' and 'ambitious yet intimate, defiantly personal yet gleefully universal'.[55] The media interest peaked when *Amelie* premiered around October and November. In addition to the positive publicity coming from Europe, the film may also have owed some of its success to the general state of mind of the American public, only weeks after the shock of September 11th, as a short article published in *USA Today* before the release of the film suggests: 'This is the kind of humorous and romantic story the world needs after Sept. 11. It is about caring for others first, which has become important, especially in New York.'[56] The campaign was orchestrated around the feel-good tone of the film and the iconic image of Audrey Tautou, who made the cover of *Time Out* in New York but declined television interviews. The French press followed this success closely with headlines such as 'French Amélie Poulain Brings a little Dream to New York'.[57]

The unquestionable success of *Amelie* in Britain and America sometimes partially conceals a less than unanimous critical reception. The emphasis in many positive reviews was placed on the feel-good, whimsical tone of the film, praising its dazzling visual style and Tautou's remarkable performance:

> The movie is a genuine triumph for Jeunet, and a daring change of pace. His previous films, for all their stylistic innovations, had been cold, mechanical and studio-bound. Here he displays an infectious joy in the simple things of life, a delightful flair for screwball comedy and a true romantic's faith in the infinite possibilities of the human heart.[58]

In addition to referring to Jeunet's previous films as a label of quality, American reviews also tended to anticipate a positive public reception as this example illustrates:

> It's also tough to imagine American audiences not falling hard for *Amélie*. Directed – or rather, choreographed – with unflagging verve by *Delicatessen*'s Jean-Pierre Jeunet, it speaks the universal language of fantasy, purveying the desire to reconfigure reality by aiding the victims and smiting the villains.[59]

However, a few critics echoed some of the reservations voiced in France concerning the excessive rosy tone of the film and its lack of warmth, such as the influential Kenneth Turan in the *L.A. Times*: '*Amelie* is what happens when a filmmaker with nasty habits tries to make nice. [...] It features an aggressive in your face romanticism that's noticeably lacking in genuine warmth.' Turan deplored the fact that the film was 'irritatingly insistent on pushing its hollow charm as if it were the real thing'.[60] Such reservations concerning lack of substance were echoed by the regret that the film encouraged passive viewership: 'The film insists on its audience's adoration while making no demands upon their intelligence.'[61] In Britain, the press focused on the Frenchness of the film and on Tautou's performance. More surprisingly, a few articles that preceded the release of the film expressed doubts about its effect on British audiences.[62]

Amelie's international success illustrates French cinema's ability to travel the world for new markets. In 2001 and 2002, the film toured the established international Festival circuit, which represents a crucial international showcase for French cinema, representing France in major film festivals, including Edinburgh, Montréal and Toronto (see Table 4 in Appendix 2). *Amelie* was awarded a record number of prizes worldwide and was nominated for the Oscars, which should not be underestimated: it not only ensured a wider release of the film, but provided a showcase for French cinema and a further opportunity to prolong the theatrical distribution of the film.

The continued life of the film

The film was officially released in France on DVD and VHS on 9 January 2002 by TF1 videos. However, a limited edition 'collector's item' had been available as early as 17 December 2001, in time for Christmas, and only eight months after the film's release. It was presented in a square tin box, reminiscent of old biscuit containers, and of Bretodeau's treasure box, which perpetuated the playful retro spirit of the film. It contained a double DVD, the soundtrack CD, a 20-page booklet relating Amélie's adventures and introducing the film's characters. There was also an envelope addressed to her father with the garden gnome's photographs, and another with stills from the film and a signed poster.

Two other DVD products were available: a single DVD edition including Jeunet's commentary and a double DVD including many special features. Apart from teasers and trailers, posters, test scenes with the actors, there were storyboard samples, a 'making-of' documentary, and extracts of a public screening discussion. It also featured Jeunet's short film *Foutaises*, which in many ways echoes and prefigures *Amelie*, and a 26-minute interview with the director analysing the film's genesis, its production contexts and its reception.

Amelie's original soundtrack containing 20 tracks was released in April 2001, followed by a limited-edition version including four extra pieces before Christmas 2001. The CD was an immediate commercial hit with 200,000 copies sold by July 2001, reaching 600,000 by July 2002.[63] It was nominated for a BAFTA award and received a César and a *Victoire de la musique* for Best Film Soundtrack in 2002. Since the success of *Amelie*, which contributed to the extension of his fan base and accelerated his mainstream recognition, Yann Tiersen has confirmed his success with another high-profile original soundtrack for *Goodbye Lenin* (2002), and international tours and special concerts such as those given at the Cité de la Musique in 2002, which formed the basis of a double album with guests, 'C'était ici'.

Two books were published around the film, an album and a storyboard. The first, *Le Fabuleux Album d'Amélie Poulain*, came from an idea by Phil Casoar, a friend of Jeunet's. It is neither a screenplay nor a commentary of the film, but rather it extends the pleasure generated by the film and re-creates its poetic world. It is illustrated with quaint old-fashioned documents and images such as birth certificates, old photos, period adverts and collectable objects. It provides glossy pictures from the film and offers new angles on the world of *Amelie* that complement the film's narrative, including additional biographical information on the film's characters, maps and plans of the buildings. These contribute to reinforcing the illusion of authenticity and realism that emanate from Amélie's fictitious world which played a substantial role in its success. There is also a photo novel derived from the short tribute imagined by Amélie in the film, the photographs from Nino's photo album and an original board game themed around the film and modelled on the old-fashioned 'Jeu de l'oie'. A fully illustrated storyboard book was also published in 2004 containing the storyboards designed by Luc Desportes as well as extra colour plates of key shots.

Amelie was a best-selling video/DVD title for 2002 with over a million copies sold,[64] before being broadcast on French television. Shown on pay channel Canal Plus on 4 September 2002 as part of a special Jeunet evening, the film was then programmed for its terrestrial TV premiere on France 3 on 18 December 2003. To mark the occasion, the film was followed by special interactive regional programmes involving the viewers, such as a debate on the theme of happiness in the France 3 region of Nord-Picardie. According to the CNC, this first broadcast attracted 10.5 million viewers, which corresponds to a 23 per cent market share.[65] In Britain, Amelie was first screened on Sky Movies, and, more significantly, its terrestrial premiere on Channel Four was programmed in primetime on 25 December 2003 (subtitled), which confirms the wide-ranging appeal of the film.

The film has regenerated the image of Montmartre, but this has been a mixed blessing for residents. House prices have risen, although this can only partly be attributed to the Amelie effect. In the wake of the film's success, fans started to retrace Amélie's steps to discover the real locations where the film had been filmed, which prompted the local tourist office to print a map clearly highlighting the various high spots (metro stations, café and Collignon's grocery). This inspired many foreign tour operators to include an 'Amelie trail' when coming to Paris, while newspapers including the New York Times and USA Today published feature articles focusing on the attractions of post-Amelie Montmartre.[66] Jumping on the bandwagon, the city of Paris sponsored open-air summer film screenings on the 'butte Montmartre'. Shown in August 2002, Amelie proved a popular event.

After Amelie, Jeunet received and declined numerous offers, ranging from an American television series to a new rose variety being named after the film.[67] Although he tried to stop parodies of Amelie from invading the French advertising market, several adverts appeared on British television, which were clearly inspired by the film: for example, the theme of the Ford Focus Edge commercial film made in 2004 is based on the altruistic values of helping others (obliteration of graffiti, helping an old lady, opening an umbrella). Its slogan 'generously equipped' and its dreamy music all recall the atmosphere of the film. Similarly, the film for Standard Life Insurance, shown in 2004, recalls Amelie with a girlish voiceover, bright colours, a surreal atmosphere and a special effect in the sky.

Other commercial businesses used *Amelie*'s image for their marketing strategies. In May 2003, the designer Lancel introduced an 'Amélie' line including clothes, bags, umbrellas, wallets, shoes, but officially disclaimed any connection with the film, even though their publicity leaflet used a slim, dark-haired model posing with the clothes and accessories. Patterned with red and black naively drawn icons of Parisian landmarks, this stylish yet unusual line was displayed in the shops' windows for several months, providing attractive souvenirs for fans and tourists alike. In 2004, Amélie's face appeared on Coca Cola bottle labels as part of the 'Filmfest 2004' promotion,[68] which offered free film tickets and organised a vote to choose the best recent films. *Amelie* was included in the shortlists. In 2005, the marketing campaign for the 'Paris 2012' Olympic Games bid used distinctive shots of Paris reminding viewers of *Amelie* and Yann Tiersen's soundtrack.

To what extent these direct and indirect exploitations of the film's image alter its identity or contribute to its continued life is difficult to say. In the case of a playful film like *Amelie*, it could even be read as an extension of the treasure hunt motif of the narrative. Whether it transforms a small French film into a 'high concept' product is another matter. While *Amelie* was first marketed as a personal film, its success revived a trend for nostalgic films inspired by chance chains of events, featuring retro motifs. A few European films were made in subsequent years, which were considered as direct *Amelie* offsprings, such as *Jeux d'enfants* (Yann Samuell, 2003) or *Goodbye Lenin* (2003). This is an ironical subversion of the main premise of the Hollywood model of 'high concept film', which consists of selling a film on an original idea, before it is even made, rather than setting a trend retrospectively.

Detailing the reception of *Amelie* at home and abroad has highlighted a number of paradoxes, but above all, it has conclusively demonstrated the elusive nature of the circumstances that turn a film into a phenomenon or transform it into the object of broader critical or political debates. It is easy to imagine why the success of the film may have led to the temptation of further exploring the '*Amelie*' concept, but it has to be said that no direct sequel was ever envisaged. However, *Un long dimanche de fiançailles*, which reunited Jeunet and Tautou in 2004, inevitably brought comparisons with *Amelie* despite its different period setting in the First World War and topic.

Post-*Amelie: Un long dimanche de fiançailles*

Three years elapsed between *Amelie* and Jeunet's next film, *Un long dimanche de fiançailles*, a 45 million euros ($57 m) Warner production, the second biggest budget for a 'French' film after *Astérix: Mission Cléopâtre* (Euros 49 m). The film was released in October 2004, following a much-publicised controversy on the legitimacy of its benefiting from the French public subsidy system in view of its being produced by an American major.[69] Yet irrespective of the 'nationality' of its budget, the film was made in French, and shot on location in France, with French actors and technicians, including the 2,500 extras. It almost regrouped the same French team as for *Amelie*, if we leave aside a different music composer (Angelo Badalamenti) and a new first assistant.

Adapted from Sébastien Japrisot's novel in collaboration with Guillaume Laurant, the film is set around the First World War. It features some realistic war scenes and re-creates the Paris of the 1920s (Place de l'Opéra, Les Halles). The now familiar cast including Tautou, Pinon, Dussolier, Dreyfus, Holgado were joined by new actors, some well established, such as Tcheky Karyo, Jean-Pierre Darroussin and Denis Lavant, some newcomers noticed in recent French films (Gaspard Ulliel, Marion Cotillard, Albert Dupontel, Jean-Paul Rouve, Julie Depardieu and Clovis Cornillac), not forgetting Jodie Foster in a guest-star cameo role.

At first glance, *Un long dimanche de fiançailles* seems quite a different project from Amelie. And yet, its heroine Mathilde has been nicknamed Amélie's grandmother and a girl 'with a velvet heart and an iron will'.[70] Some visual effects of the film directly recall *Amelie*. 'I had to restrain myself and leave out some of the visual ideas that I had because it would have looked too much like *Amelie*,' Jeunet replies.[71]

Meeting the inevitable pressure to match *Amelie*'s success, *Un long dimanche de fiançailles* was marketed as one of the events of 2004, and was seen by 1.6 million viewers in its first week, with a total of 4.5 million in France alone. This did not match *Amelie*, but certainly reaffirmed Jeunet's directorial talent and his international status. He was approached in 2004 to direct the fifth episode of the *Harry Potter* series. He finally declined this high-profile but constrictive commission, and a chance to re-access the globalised pole of cinema. He has since been associated with Fox 2000 for another American film project, based on Yann Martell's fantasy novel and Booker Prize winner, *The Life of Pi*.

Amelie has had a lasting impact on Audrey Tautou's international career. After *Un long dimanche de fiançailles* and films in English made with Amos Gitai and Stephen Frears, she has been cast alongside Tom Hanks for another Hollywood blockbuster of 2006, adapted from Dan Brown's bestseller *The Da Vinci Code*, set in Paris, France.

Notes

1   Lefort, G. and D. Péron, 'Je ne suis pas prêt de revivre un tel miracle', *Libération*, 26 December 2001, pp.21–22.

2   See Cinemondial statistics site on website, http://www.cinemondial.com/detailfilm. php?numfilm=73, accessed 21 December 2004.

3   See the critical controversy around Patrice Leconte's open letter in 1999 mentioned in Chapter One, or Dupeyron's interview for the release of *Inguelezi* in A. de Baecque, 'Dupeyron dans la clandestinité', *Libération*, 26 May 2004.

4   S. Waskiewicz, 'Le Fabuleux destin d'Amélie Poulain', *French Politics Culture and Society* 20. 1, pp.152–155.

5   See R. Baronian, 'Cinéma, nouvelle vague... marketing', *L'Expansion,* 1 February 2002. Luc Besson had also used these Hollywood marketing strategies for his films.

6   Quoted in *Variety*, 20 August 2001, p.7.

7   M. Kandel, 'Les fabuleuses recettes d'Amélie Poulain', *Le Point*, 11 May 2001, p.76. Blockbusters like *La vérité si je mens 2* had 2.2 million viewers with 827 screens, *Taxi 3* had 3 million with 800 screens.

8   For example, Phil Powrie's book *French Cinema in the 1990s* (Oxford: Oxford University Press, 1999) highlighted nostalgia represented as a central motif in the French cinema of that period. Nostalgia is a component of Jeunet and Caro's world, yet Powrie only mentions Jeunet briefly in his introduction as an example – with Luc Besson – of a film-maker attracted by a 'transatlantic crossover' (p.20). Similarly, Jeunet and Caro were absent from the collection of essays edited by Lucy Mazdon, *France on Film: Reflections on French Popular Cinema* (London: Wallflower, 2000).

9   G. Austin, *Contemporary French Cinema* (Manchester: Manchester University Press, 1996), p.135; see also a brief association of Jeunet and Caro with *cinéma du look* in A. Smith, '*Nikita* as social fantasy' in *France on Film*, 2002 (pp.22-25). Mazdon (ed.), 2001, p.27.

10   See for example Lavoignat: *Studio Magazine* 158 (July 2000), pp.12–17.

11   For examples see Vincendeau's press review in 'Café society' (2001), but also various articles published in the French press in April 2001, such as F. Garbarz in *Positif* (2001), O. De Bruyn in *Le Point* (2001), J.-C. Loiseau in *Télérama*.

12   T. Sotinel, 'Le Fabuleux destin d'Amélie Poulain: quand Georges Perec rencontre Marcel Carné', *Le Monde*, 24 April 2001; D. Péron and J.-M. Lalanne, 'Un coup de Jeunet', *Libération*, 25 April 2001.

13   M. Boujut, 'Destins contrariés', *Charlie Hebdo*, 2 May 2001, V. Ostria, 'Le Fabuleux destin d'Amélie Poulain', *L'Humanité*, 25 April 2001, and F. Gorin, 'Arbitraire', *Télérama*, 25 April 2001. Other examples include C.-M. Trémois, 'Le sinistre destin d'Amélie Poulain', '*Esprit* 278 (October 2001), pp.194–196, published a few months after the release of the film.

14   See, for example, an article in *Le Monde* (Belleret, 2001) in which the reaction of viewers coming out of the film is analysed.

15   J.-P. Lavoignat, '2001 ou le triomphe du cinéma français' and 'Jean-Pierre Jeunet: ce qui m'arrive est exceptionnel', *Studio Magazine* Hors Série, December 2001, pp.54–73. G. Lefort and D Péron: *Libération*, 26 December 2001. C. Mulard and T. Sotinel, 'Amélie Poulain, un tour du monde en 17 millions d'entrées', *Le Monde*, 1 January 2002.

16   J.-M. Frodon, 'Une chevauchée fantastique sans pareil', *Le Monde*, 1 January 2002, p.24.

17   According to *Marianne*, nearly one million viewers participated in internet forum discussions on the film and 99.9 per cent of the comments were positive (Dupont-Monod, Jaillette and Kaplan, 'La France d'Amélie Poulain contre la France de Loft Story', *Marianne* 212, 14 May 2001).

18   See, for example, Frodon: 2002, p.24.

19   France was at the time in a situation of 'cohabitation', with a right-wing president and a socialist government.

20   G. Bresson, R. Dely and D. Hassoux, 'Un besoin de bonheur simple' and D. Péron, 'Quatre millions d'adhérents au parti d'Amélie Poulain', *Libération*, 2 June 2001.

21   Jeunet, quoted in Vincendeau: 2001, p.25.

22   Vincendeau: 2001, p.25.

23   Frodon: 2002, p.24.

24   G. Kenny, '*Amelie*', *US Premiere*, November 2001, pp.90–91.

25   J. Larcher, 'Le cabinet des curiosités', *Cahiers du cinéma*, May 2001, p.112.

26   Vincendeau: 2001, p.25.

27   A typical example is the contribution of Frédéric Mitterrand, an emblematic figure of cinephile culture on French television to narrate the fake tribute to Amélie Poulain.

28   B. Gurrey, 'Quand Chirac décore le réalisateur d'Amélie Poulain', *Le Monde*, 24 October 2002.

29 Austin: 2004, p.284.
30 R. Belleret, 'Le Rendez-vous manqué du festival de Cannes', *Le Monde*, 6 May 2001; O. Séguret, 'Cannes, son délit d'Amélie', *Libération*, 9 May 2001.
31 D. Martin-Castelnau and G. Bigot, 'Le secret d'Amélie Poulain', *Libération*, 28 May 2001. The article argued that the film's success rested on its representation of ordinary French people, and deplored the elitism displayed by the few negative reviews that it received.
32 See C. Andrews, 'The social ageing of *Les Inrockuptibles*', *French Cultural Studies* 11. 2 (32), June 2000, pp.235–248.
33 S. Kaganski, 'Amélie pas jolie', *Libération*, 31 May 2001.
34 S. Kaganski, 'Le septième artifice', *Les Inrockuptibles*, 7 May 1995, p.38.
35 Kaganski: 2001; see also Austin: 2004, pp.290–292.
36 See, for example, the review in *L'Humanité*, which situates the film in 'a postcard Montmartre presumably aimed at seducing the American audience fond of the picturesque' (Ostria: 2001, translated by and quoted in Vincendeau: 2001, p.23).
37 See *Libération*'s website and an article 'le parti d'Amélie', dated 4 June 2001. The numerous letters of complaint sent to *Les Inrockuptibles* prompted a response by Kaganski, 'Pourquoi je n'aime pas Amélie Poulain', in *Les Inrockuptibles*, 11 June 2001. Several articles were published in *Libération* in the first week of June, including Lançon, 'Le frauduleux destin d'Amélie Poulain', 1 June 2001, and Péron: 2001.
38 Lançon: 1 June 2001.
39 V. Thomas and C. Le Caro's editorial open letter 'Etat critique d'une critique', Website http://www.ecrannoir.fr., accessed on 25 June 2003. See also D. Parent, 'Parenthèse', *Studio Magazine* 169 (July 2001), p.10; D. Jamet, 'Messieurs les censeurs, gardez vos munitions', *Marianne*, 11 June 2001; T. Sotinel, 'Amélie et la boîte aux fantasmes', *Le Monde*, 8 June 2001; J. Lichfield, 'French elite horrified as feel good film seduces nation', *Independent*, 2 June 2001, p.15, also published in *Le Courrier international* in French, 21 June 2001, p.15.
40 See particularly Kaganski's review of this film in *Les Inrockuptibles* (4 September 2001) and the special dossier and interview in *Cahiers du cinéma*, 559 (July 2001), pp.41–58. Unfortunately we do not have the space here to develop this comparison, which could include the treatment of other *auteur* French films of the same year such as *Va savoir* (Rivette) and popular spectacles such as *Moulin Rouge* (Luhrman).
41 Séguret: 2001.
42 See for example Lichfield: 2001, p.15. This argument is developed in a paper by Ingrid Stiggdotter, 'Very funny if you can keep up with the subtitles: The reception of *Le Fabuleux destin d'Amélie Poulain*', given at the 'Issues in Contemporary Popular Cinema' in Manchester in January 2006.
43 S. Jeffries, 'The French insurrection', *Observer*, 24 June 2001; F. Bonnaud, 'The Amelie effect', *Film Comment* 37, 6 (November/December 2001), pp. 36–38; and Vincendeau: 2001, pp. 22-25.
44 A. Campion, 'Jean-Pierre Jeunet, le miracle d'Amélie et le "goût de chiotte absolu"', *Journal du dimanche*, 12 August 2001.
45 *Loft Story* attracted 4 million viewers every night and 6 million for the weekly primetime (Dupont-Monod, Jaillette and Kaplan: 2001.
46 See V. Remy, 'Amélie nous lie', *Télérama*, 16 May 2001; J.M. Helvig, 'L'Anti-Loana', *Libération*, 2 June 2001; D. Zerbib, 'Amélie sortie du loft', *Humanité*, 12 June 2001; and Roux: 2001, pp.64–65.
47 She ended up winning the game, and published her autobiography in 2002, which immediately became a bestseller.
48 It later transpired that her physical assets were partly the result of plastic surgery and that she had withheld information about her past and her child.
49 P. Escande and M. Esquirou, 'Claudie Ossard: les films que je fais sont ceux que j'aime', *Les Echos*, 17 May 2001.

50   *Film français*, 2926, 8 March 2002. Six hundred articles were devoted to *Amelie*, and it benefited from a two-month promotional campaign. The success of *Amelie* Paris tours is another sign of the impact of the film.

51   Source: IMDb box office data.

52   *Amelie*'s success was only matched by *Le Cinquième Élément* (Besson, 1997) but the film had major stars Bruce Willis, was shot in English and its style was largely inspired by American science fiction and action films. $33.2 million takings is a relative commercial success if compared with surprise home hit *Blair Witch Project* and its $242 million gross takings, or the $128 million of *Wo hu cang long/Crouching Tiger, Hidden Dragon* (Ang Lee, 2000).

53   Benigni's film won three Oscars and grossed a record $57 m in the US. Miramax's intentions were reported in *Variety* as early as 20 August 2001 (A. Dawtrey and A. James, 'Guarded Gauls brace for Miramax march', p.7).

54   For information on the film's US release, see anon., 'Miramax reveal *Amelie* Oscar strategy', *Guardian*, 5 November 2001, V. Le Leurch, 'Jeunet en justes noces avec Warner Independent', *Film français*, 22 October 2004.

55   L. Nesselson, '*Amelie from Montmartre*', *Variety*, 30 April 2001, p.26.

56   C. Bell, '*Amelie* capturing world fancy', *USA Today*, 1 November 2001. See also R. Corliss, 'Affairs of the Heart', *Time*, 12 November 2001.

57   A. Cojean, *Le Monde*, 6 November 2001. See, for example, J. Lichfield, 'Amelie bestows cash and chaos on Paris', *Independent*, 27 October 2001, p.11; E. Sciolino, 'Cinematography meets geography in Montmartre', *New York Times*, 10 August 2003.

58   W. Arnold, 'Inspired *Amelie* blends solid comedy with cutting edge special effects', *Seattle Post-Intelligencer*, 9 November 2001.

59   Abee, E., 'Amelie', *International Film Journal*, 2001. See also Kempley: 2001.

60   K. Turan, 'Mean streak hurts *Amelie*', *Los Angeles Times*, 2 November 2001.

61   M. Dargis, 'Sleepless in Montmartre', *LA Weekly*, 2 November 2001.

62   For example, P. Preston: 2001; Quinn: 2001, p.10.

63   World Wide Web 'pianart' http://www.webzinemaker.com, accessed on 21 December 2004.

64   *CNC info*, 289 (January 2004), p.17.

65   This is less than *Astérix et Obélix: Mission Cléopâtre* or *Monsieur Batignole* (Jugnot, 2002), which both had over 12 million viewers in 2004. A second terrestrial primetime broadcast on 25 October 2005 on France 2 confirmed the ongoing interest for the film with over 6 million viewers (source: Mediamétrie surveys).

66   E. Sciolino, 'Cinematography meets geography in Montmartre', *New York Times*, 10 August 2003 and Walt: 2001. See also Lichfield: 2001, p.11.

67   In Lefort and Péron: 2001.

68   See website www.coke.filmfest.com, accessed 23 October 2004.

69   The French production majors challenged the accreditation of the film by the CNC in 2003, querying the status of production company '2003 productions', a subsidiary of Warner France funded by American money and specially created for the production of French films. For more details, see N. Vulser, 'Des Producteurs contestent les aides publiques accordées au film', *Le Monde*, 26 October 2004; F. Priot, *Financement et devis des films français* (Paris: Dixit, 2005), pp. 141–207.

70   Jeunet in Libiot: 19 January 2004.

71   Rouyer and Vassé: 2004, p. 9.

Conclusion: *Amelie* and cultural diversity

Within a period of five years, *Amelie* has acquired a prominent place in French cinema that extends beyond the box office smash hit, veering towards its consecration as modern classic. The emphasis that was placed in this study on the director as the 'Maestro', orchestrating the work of creation, was not accidental. Jeunet was ever-present at all levels of the film's life from its conception, production, to the marketing and even in its afterlife. After *Alien: Resurrection*, Jeunet had 'renounced the global [...] returning with affection to the local'.[1] In other words, he had opted for the French cultural exception and 'more artistic freedom' rather than the globalised Hollywood production values. After *Amelie*, the Hollywood temptation returned.

Beyond changing the lives of those who contributed to its making, *Amelie* has reopened a broader debate about new directions in French cinema, mapping its future in the context of the globalisation of culture. If *Amelie*'s global success can be partly explained by its ability to seduce audiences with 'universal' values and accessible subject matter, the film can also be read as a response to the domination of a formatted American cinema, which is ironic if we consider that it was made by one of the few French directors to have successfully worked in Hollywood. Whereas *Amelie* did embrace some of the new technologies that contribute to the domination of American productions worldwide, it also created a spectacle that attractively retained its French cultural identity. Discussing this very point, the review *Positif* proposed a symbolic reading of the film which is revealing:

> The success of *Amelie* [...] offers the image of a France that is still little prepared for globalisation, a France jealous of its economic and cultural exception, preoccupied by the unstable economy, and shaken by the consequences of giving up the French franc. It relieves its fears by opting for the pleasures of infantile regression, which can be a good thing if it remains reasonable.[2]

This interpretation of *Amelie* as a feel-good, regressive object of reassurance is typical of the condescending critical reaction to French popular successes, but is not necessarily applied by the same critics when it comes to discussing American fantasy genres, say for example Tim Burton's films.

If we develop this argument a little further, Amélie Poulain could be the female alter-ego of yet another emblematic French character, Astérix the little Gaul who set out to defy the Roman Empire. If the two characters set out to conquer the world and resist the pressures of dominant cultures, there is a significant difference in the reception of the two films: *Astérix and Obélix: Mission Cléopâtre* may have attracted a record 15 million viewers into French cinemas in 2002, beating all the American blockbusters of that year, but it did not attract international audiences, probably because of the profusion of specific cultural references underlying its comic effects that were inaccessible to non-French audiences. Jeunet's achievement (and *Amelie*'s strength) was to meet the challenge of accessibility, while attracting French viewers of all generations and social backgrounds as well as large numbers of viewers through the world, a feat rarely achieved by French films.

How representative is Jeunet's cinema of new trends in French cinema? The success of *Amelie*, as many critics noted, was a combination of aesthetic and commercial elements. It ensured Jeunet unlimited financial credit and artistic freedom for his next films, while reviving the desire of the majors to work with him.[3] *Amelie* promoted a romantic vision of film-making as a craftsman's activity, which is not without paradoxes. It combined a personal conception cinema with ambitions of popular success. It was turned towards the past, but relied on state-of-the-art technology and spectacular effects. It blended cultural specificity and the universal, thus repositioning the future of French cinema in the debate of globalised cinema versus cultural diversity.[4] When *Amelie* was released, Glenn Kenny went as far as to state that 'at a time when Hollywood is squandering its monopoly on moviemaking magic, Jeunet cast a wicked spell from across the pond all the while doing it the French way'.[5] With the release of his new film in 2004, Jeunet may well have moved even closer to a new form of cultural diversity, distinct from Hollywood, but no longer strictly defined by its nationality.

Notes

1   Andrew: 2004, p.34.
2   Roux: 2001, p.65.
3   In 2004, he declined the offer to direct the fifth Harry Potter film.
4   'Cultural diversity' has been increasingly used in France recently to replace 'cultural exception, which was considered too aggressive. See B. Gournay, *Exception culturelle et mondialisation* (Paris: Presse de Science Po, 2002), back cover summary.
5   Kenny: 2001, p.91.

Appendix 1: Full credits

Director: Jean-Pierre Jeunet

Writing credits:
Screenplay: Jean-Pierre Jeunet and Guillaume Laurant
Dialogue: Guillaume Laurant

Cast (in credits order):

Audrey Tautou	Amélie Poulain
Mathieu Kassovitz	Nino Quincampoix
Rufus	Raphaël Poulain, Amélie's father
Lorella Cravotta	Amandine Poulain
Serge Merlin	Raymond Dufayel
Jamel Debbouze	Lucien
Clotilde Mollet	Gina
Claire Maurier	Suzanne
Isabelle Nanty	Georgette
Dominique Pinon	Joseph
Artus de Penguern	Hipolito
Yolande Moreau	Madeleine Wallace
Urbain Cancelier	Collignon
Maurice Bénichou	Bretodeau
Michel Robin	Mr Collignon
Andrée Damant	Mrs Collignon
Claude Perron	Eva
Armelle	Philomène
Ticky Holgado	Man in photo
Kevin Fernandes	Bretodeau (child)
Flora Guiet	Amélie (child)
Amaury Babault	Nino (child)
André Dussollier	Narrator
Eugène Berthier	Eugene Koler
Marion Pressburger	Credits helper
Charles-Roger Bour	The urinal man
Luc Palun	Amandine's grocer
Fabienne Chaudat	Woman in coma
Dominique Bettenfeld	The screaming neighbour
Jacques Viala	The customer who humiliates his friend
Fabien Béhar	The humiliated customer
Jonathan Joss	The humiliated customer's son
Jean-Pierre Becker	The beggar
Jean Darie	The blind man
Thierry Gibault	The endive client
François Bercovici	His friend

Franck Monier	Dominique Bredoteau (child)
Guillaume Viry	The vagrant
Valérie Zarrouk	Dominique Bredoteau (woman)
Marie-Laure Descoureaux	The dead man's concierge
Sophie Tellier	Aunt Josette
Gérald Weingand	The teacher
François Viaur	The bar owner
Paule Daré	His employee
Marc Amyot	The stranger
Myriam Labbé	The tobacco buyer
Jean Rupert	Nasal operation man
Frankie Pain	The news-stand woman
Julianna Kovacs	Grocer's client
Philippe Paimblanc	Train ticket taker
Mady and Monette Malroux	The twins
Robert Gendreu	Café patron
Valériane de Villeneuve	The laughing woman
Isis Peyrade	Samantha
Raymonde Heudeline	Ghost-train customer
Christiane Bopp	Woman at the merry-go-round
Thierry Arfeuillères	Statue man
Jerry Lucas	The Sacré-Coeur boy
Patrick Paroux	The street prompter
François Aubineau	The concierge's postman
Philippe Beautier	Poulain's postman
Karine Asure	Pretty girl at appointment
Régis Iacono	Félix L'Herbier
Franck-Olivier Bonnet	Palace Video (voice)
Alain Floret	The concierge's husband (voice)
Jean-Pol Brissart	The postman (voice)
Frédéric Mitterrand	Himself (voice)
Manoush	Nymphomaniac woman

Production:

Jean-Marc Deschamps	producer
Arne Meerkamp van Embden	producer: Germany
Claudie Ossard	executive producer/producer

Original music: Yann Tiersen
Non-original music: Samuel Barber (from 'Adagio for Strings')

Cinematography: Bruno Delbonnel

Film editing: Hervé Schneid

Casting: Pierre-Jacques Bénichou; Valerie Espagne; Alberte Garo

Production design: Aline Bonetto

Art direction: Volker Schäfer

Set decoration: Marie-Laure Valla

Costume design: Madeline Fontaine; Emma Lebail

Make-up department:

Véronique Boitout	hair stylist
Reynald Desbant	hair stylist
Virginie Duranteau	hair stylist
Vesna Estord	make-up artist
Dominique Galichet	make-up artist
Karina Gruais	make-up artist
John Nollet	key hair stylist
Myriam Roger	hair stylist
Nathalie Tissier	key make-up artist

Production management:

Nicolas Davy	assistant unit manager
Jean-Marc Deschamps	production manager
Eric Duchêne	unit manager
Marc Grewe	unit production manager
Alain Mougenot	unit production manager

Second unit director or assistant director:

Thomas Parnet	trainee assistant director
Pascal Roy	second assistant director
Christophe Vassort	first assistant director

Art department:

Jean-Marc Auriol	painter
Michèle Bataille	painter: 'Renoir–Le déjeuner des canotiers'
Karin Beizler	painter: Cologne
Jörg Bergen	props: Germany
Britta Bogers	painter: Cologne
François Borgeaud	propman
Pascale Bouillot	painter: 'Renoir–Le déjeuner sur l'herbe'
Claudin Brackhagen	painter: Cologne
Reiner Brüggen	carpenter: Cologne
Wolfgang Gosberg	carpenter: Cologne
Alain Guais	dressing props
Gregor Hees	carpenter: Cologne
Herbert Hees	sculptor: Cologne
Daniel Kolarov	assistant art director
Kerstin Krötz	props: Germany
Delphine Mabed	first assistant art director: Germany
Fabrice Maux	chief painter
Anja Merz	carpenter: Cologne
Jacques Pélissier	art department assistant
Jörn Quel	carpenter: Cologne
Stefan Quentin	construction coordinator: Germany
John Rawsthorn	carpenter: Cologne
Hélène Rey	art department trainee
Thorsten Sabel	set dresser: Cologne
Lorenzo Sartor	carpenter: Cologne
Britta Sassmannshausen	painter: Cologne
Ralf Schwamborn	props: Germany
Volker Schäfer	set decorator: Cologne
Nane Stegat	painter: Cologne
Marie-Laure Valla	set buyer
Dagmar Wessel	set dresser: Cologne

Sound department:

Jean-Philippe Angelini	post-synchronisation assistant
Vincent Arnardi	sound re-recording mixer
Marilena Cavola	sound editor
Sophie Chiabaut	sound
Stéphane De Rocquigny	post-synchronisation assistant
Michel Filippi	post-synchronisation engineer
Gérard Hardy	sound editor
Laurent Kossayan	sound effects
Jean-Louis Lebras	boom operator
Jean-Pierre Lelong	sound effects editor
Guillaume Leriche	sound re-recording mixer
Mario Melchiorri	assistant sound effects editor
Franck Mettre	sound mixer
Igor Thomas-Gerard	assistant sound editor
Jean Umansky	sound
Alexandre Widmer	sound editor

Special effects:

Jean-Baptiste Bonetto	special effects
Noël Chaimbaux	special effects
Solena Collignon	digital special effects
Séverine De Wever	special effects coordinator
Yves Domenjoud	special effects supervisor
Olivier Gleyze	special effects
Delphine Le Roch	special effects coordinator
Daniel Lenoir	special effects
Marc Paccosi	digital special effects
Thierry Reymonenq	special effects
Jean-Christophe Spadaccini	special effects: second unit
Edouard Valton	special effects production manager

Visual effects:

Christophe Belena	I/O technician and scanning and conforming technician
Lucie Bories	digital compositor
Andre Brizard	digital compositor
Alain Carsoux	visual effects supervisor
Stéphanie Dargent	digital matte painter
Thierry Delobel	digital compositor
Stephane Dittoo	digital artist
François Dupuy	digital processing technician
Thomas Duval	shooting supervisor
Xavier Fourmond	compositing supervisor
Afif Heukeshoven	3D artist
Rovela Jean-Paul	3D supervisor
Alexandre Kolasinski	digital compositor
Bruno Le Provost	digital matte painter
Jeremie Leroux	digital artist
Tina Lin	scanning and conforming technician
Olivier Revillon	digital matte painter
Antoine Simkine	visual effects executive producer: Duboi
Michael Sowa	matte painter
Georges Tornero	digital compositor

Daniel Trujillo	digital compositor
Daniel Trujillo	digital effects artist
Pierre Villette	digital matte painter
Jean-Marie Vives	digital matte painter
Veronique Zylberfain	matte painting artist
Didier le Fouest	colorist and digital grading

Stunts:

Rémi Canaple	stunts
Patrick Cauderlier	stunts
Pascaline Girardot	stunts
Jean-Claude Lagniez	stunt driver
Sébastien Lagniez	stunt driver
Sébastien Seveau	stunt driver

Other crew:

Aurore Ader	digital laboratory assistant
Werner Ahrendt	driver
Christophe Antonin	unit assistant
Matthieu Bastid	first assistant camera
Chantal Bégasse	production secretary
Sylvie Bello	assistant costumer
Stéphane Bourdon	weapons
Thomas Brügge	electrician: Germany
Bruno Calvo	still photographer
Gilles Caussade	financial director
Olivier Cazzitti	electrician
Laurent Clavier	research and development
Dominique Colin	camera operator
Christophe Colter	transfer technician
Marie-Laure Compain	production secretary
Kenneth Cornils	best boy grip: Germany
Deborah Coucoux	digital processing trainee
Clémentine Darros	trainee costumer
Frédéric Daugeron	party organiser
Stefan de Leuw	assistant camera: Germany
Olivier Delpy	grip
Patrick de Ranter	steadicam operator
Luc Desportes	trainee
Stephane Deverly	research and development
Robert Dona	grip
Bruno Dubet	key grip
Edouard Dubois	musical advisor
Eric Dupressoir	grip
Jean-Christophe Duwez	electrician
Véronique Élise	assistant costumer
Sébastien Guyomard	technician
Rip Hampton O'Neil	director of technology
Nicole Heitzmann	production administrator
Alexandre Jeanneret	digital processing technician
Abdel Ali Kassou	digital processing technician
Céline Kélépikis	assistant editor
Lionel Kopp	director of post-production

Vlasta Kostic	electrician: Germany
Georgi Lazarevski	assistant camera
Aude Lemercier	location scout
Dominique Lepage	grip
Yvan Lucas	35 mm calibration
Yann Malcor	assistant editor
Christophe Maratier	weapons
Beatrice Mizrahi	director of photography: second unit
Sophie Mollard	electrician
Eva Neufahrt	accountant
Nicolas Nicole	digital processing trainee
Frank Niemann	intern: Germany
Svetlana Novak	production assistant
François Paumard	assistant camera
Christophe Perotin	second assistant camera
Michel Sabourdy	chief electrician
Isabelle Sauvanon	press attaché
Torsten Schneider	intern: Germany
Thomas Sidopoulos	grip
Ludovic Simeon	video assistant
Jacques Smerlak	executive producer: music
Robert Spina	intern: Germany
Joel Spinola	electrician
Laurent Thiery	grip
Thierry Tronchet	assistant camera
Olivier Tubach	research and development
Patricia Van	casting assistant
Sophie Vermersch	post-production assistant
Tommaso Versallo	director: digital laboratory
Timo von Burgsdorf	electrician: Germany
Anne Wermelinger	script supervisor
Jörg Widmer	steadicam operator

Appendix 2: Statistics and tables

Table 1: Box office for Top 20 French films released in 2001

(Source CNC, Bilan 2001, 283, May 2002, p.7)

Title, Director and Genre	Nationality	Number of Viewers in France in Million (Rank)
Le Fabuleux destin d'Amélie Poulain (Jean-Pierre Jeunet)	Fr/Ger	8.85 (1)
La Vérité si je mens 2 (Thomas Gilou, comedy)	Fr	7.46 (2)
Le Pacte des loups (Christophe Gans, historical drama, adventure, fantastic)	Fr	5.58 (4)
Le Placard (Francis Veber, comedy)	Fr	5.29 (5)
Yamakasi (Ariel Zeitoun, action comedy)	Fr	3.22 (12)
Tanguy (Etienne Chatiliez, comedy)	Fr	3.03 (15)
Belphégor, le fantôme du Louvre (Jean-Paul Salomé, historical drama)	Fr	2.48 (20)
Un crime au paradis (Jean Becker, intimist comedy)	Fr	2.31 (21)
Une hirondelle a fait le printemps (Christian Carion, intimist drama)	Fr/Bel	2.21 (23)
La Tour Montparnasse infernale (Charles Nemes, comedy)	Fr	2.19 (25)
Vidocq (Pitof, historical adventure)	Fr	1.89 (30)
15 Août (Patrick Alessandrin, comedy)	Fr	1.59 (35)
Absolument fabuleux (Gabriel Aghion, comedy)	Fr	1.59 (36)
Les Rois mages (Didier Bourdon and Bernard Campan, comedy)	Fr	1.47 (38)
Les Visiteurs en Amérique (Jean-Marie Gaubert, comedy)	Fr	1.38 (40)
Le Baiser mortel du dragon (Chris Nahon, Action)	Fr	1.34 (43)
Chaos (Coline Serreau, comedy)	Fr	1.33 (44)
Le petit Poucet (Olivier Dahan, fairytale)	Fr	1.28 (45)
Wasabi (Gérard Krawczyk, action comedy)	Fr	1.27 (47)
Le Peuple migrateur (Jacques Perrin, documentary)	Fr/Ita	1.05 (49)

Table 2: Overall budgets and special effects budgets in context

(Sources CNC, Film français, IMDb and AlloCiné)

Film title	Overall budget	Special effects budget (number of manipulated shots)
Delicatessen (1991)	FF 24m	Not available (610 manipulated shots)
La Cité des enfants perdus (1995)	FF 90m	FF 9m (144 SFX shots)
Alien: Resurrection (1997)	FF 432m (Euro 66m) $70m	Not available (200 SFX shots)
Amelie (2001)	FF 76.68m (Euro 11.7m) $12m	FF 10.7m (123 SFX shots) FF 6.7m for sets and costumes FF 10m for technical budget
Un long dimanche de fiançailles (2004)	Euro 45m $57m	(283 SFX shots out of a total 1,300)
Vidocq (2001)	FF152m (Euro 23.2m) $30m	FF 5.1m (800 shots out of a total 2,300) FF 21m for sets and costumes.
Le Pacte des loups (2001)	FF 200m (Euro 30m) +$30m	FF 30m
Belphégor (2001)	FF 105m (Euro 16m) $14.5m	(160 SFX shots)
Astérix et Obélix: Mission Cléopâtre (2002)	FF 327m (Euro 55m)	(265 SFX shots)

Table 3: Box office

(Sources IMDb, Film Français, Ecran total, Première, CNC)

Film title	Viewers France (n° screens 1st week)	Receipts USA (n° screens)	Viewers GB (n° screens)
Amelie	8.85 m (=$40m) 125,000 1st day 1.2m 1st week (432 screens)	US $33.2m (~ 3m viewers) (335 screens max)	1m viewers (110 screens)
Vidocq	1.89 m (655 screens)	Not released	Not released
Le Pacte des loups	5.6 m (725 screens)	$10.9m (404 screens)	£123,000 (75 screens)
Astérix et Obélix: Mission Cléopâtre	14.32 m record 3.6m in 1st week (900 screens)	Not released	Not available

Film title	Viewers France (n° screens 1st week)	Receipts USA (n° screens)	Viewers GB (n° screens)
Delicatessen	+2 m	$1.7m	£1.2m
La Cité des enfants perdus	1.2m 1st week 39,000 (150 screens)	$1.5m	Not available
Alien: Resurrection	2.6m (1m 1st week) (450 screens)	$47m (2415 screens in 1st week)	£7.2m
Un Long dimanche de fiançailles	4.5 m in December 04 (1.6m 1st week) (710 screens)	$5m (January 2005) (219 screens max)	(121 screens)
La Vita è bella	4.3m	US $57m (1,136 screens after Oscars)	£3m 719,000 spect.

Table 4: Main nominations and awards for *Amelie*

(Source IMDb)

Awarding Body	Nominations	Awards
French Césars (France 2002)	Best Actress Best Supporting Actor Best Supporting Actress Best Sound Best Editing Best Screenplay Best Photography Best Costumes	Four awards: Best Film Best Director Best Soundtrack Best Set Design
Academy Awards (Oscars)	Best Foreign Film Best Art Direction-Set Decoration Best Cinematography Best Sound Best Writing Screenplay Written Directly for the Screen	
Golden Globes	Best Foreign Film	
BAFTA (Great Britain 2002)	9 Nominations	Best Screenplay Best Production Design
Lumières du cinéma français (French equivalent of Golden Globes 2002)		Best Film Best Screenplay Best Actress (Tautou)

Awarding Body	Nominations	Awards
14th European Film Awards (2002)	Best Actress	Best Film Best Director Best Photo (Delbonnel)
Bogey Awards (Germany 2001)		Bogey Award
German Arthouse Cinemas (2001)		Gold Award for Foreign Film
Donatello Awards (Italy 2002)	Best Foreign Film	
Goya Awards (2002)		Best European Film
Karlovy Vary International Film Festival (2001)		Crystal Globe
Amanda Awards (Norway 2002)		Best Foreign Feature Film
Chicago International Film Festival (2002)		Audience Choice Award
Florida Film Critics (2002)		Best Film Best Foreign Film
Denver International Film Festival (2001)		Best Fiction Film
Toronto Festival (2001)		People's Choice Award
London Critics Circle Awards (2002)		Best Foreign Film
Edinburgh International Film Festival (2001)		Audience Award (Jeunet)
Empire Awards (UK 2002)	Best Actress Best Independent Spirit (Jeunet)	
Broadcast Film Critics Association (2002)		Best Foreign Film
American Cinema Editors (2002)	Best Edited Feature Film	

Appendix 3: Jean-Pierre Jeunet's Filmography

1978   *L'Évasion/The Escape* (Jeunet and Caro)
1979   *Le Manège/The Merry-Go-Round* (Jeunet and Caro)
1981   *Le Bunker de la dernière rofale/The Last Burst Bunker* (Jeunet and Caro)
1983   *Pas de repos pour Billy Brakko/No Rest for Billy Brakko*
1989   *Foutaises/Things I Like, Things I Don't Like*
1991   *Delicatessen* (Jeunet and Caro)
1995   *La Cité des enfants perdus/The City of Lost Children* (Jeunet and Caro)
1998   *Alien: Resurrection*
2001   *Le Fabuleux destin d'Amélie Poulain/Amelie (Amelie from Montmartre)*
2004   *Un long dimanche de fiançailles/A Very long Engagement*

Appendix 4: Selected bibliography

Abee, E., 'Amelie', Film Journal International, 28 August 2001

Allion, V. (2001) 'Le Fabuleux destin d'Amélie Poulain', Avant-Scène Cinéma 502 (May 2001), pp.124–126

Andrew, D., 'Amélie or le fabuleux destin du cinéma français', Film Quarterly 57. 3 (2004), pp.34–46

Austin, J.F. (2004) 'Digitizing Frenchness in 2001: on a historic moment in the French Cinema', French Cultural Studies 15. 3 (October 2004), pp.281–299

Belleret, R.(2001) 'L'édifiante histoire du fabuleux succès d'Amélie Poulain', Le Monde, 8 May 2001

Bergery, B. (2004) 'Cinematic Impressionism', American Cinematographer, December 2004, pp.58–69

Bonnaud, F. (2001) 'The Amelie effect', Film Comment 37. 6 (November/December 2001), pp. 36–38

Calhoun, J. (2002) 'Amélie: fabricating a new French fable', Entertainment Design, 1 January 2002. World Wide Web, http://entertainmentdesignmag.com/mag/show_business_amlie fabricating_new/, accessed 3 February 2004

Chevallier, F. (2001) 'Le Fabuleux destin d'Amélie Poulain', http://www.tournages-lesite.com/pages/actualite/archives/ameliepoulain/amelie/html, accessed on 9 September 2004

Clanet, Y. and J.L. Deriaz (2001) 'Amélie from Montmartre', ARRI News 9, 2001, World Wide Web, http://www.arri.com/infodown/news/0109_e.pdf, pp.8–11, accessed on 23 April 2004.

Corliss, R. (2001) 'Affairs of the heart', Time 158. 21 (12 November 2001), pp.93–94

Dacbert, S. (2001) 'Trois réalisateurs adeptes de la simplicité…et du public', Le Film français 2911, 23 November 2001, pp. 18–19

Daunais, I., 'Le grand jeu', Inconvénient: Revue Littéraire d'Essai et de Création 8 (February 2002), pp.67–74

Deydier, C. and E. Libiot, 'Jeunet, un destin de cinéaste', Express, 19 April 2001, pp.59–60

Dupont-Monod, C., J-C. Jaillette and G. Kaplan (2001) 'La France d'Amélie Poulain contre la France de Loft Story', Marianne 212, 14 May 2001

Ezra, E. (2004) 'The death of an icon: Le Fabuleux destin d'Amélie Poulain', French Cultural Studies 13. 3 (October 2004), pp.301–310

Frodon (2002) 'Une Chevauchée fantastique sans pareil', Le Monde, 1 January 2002, p.24.

Garbarz, F. (2001) 'La Recolleuse de morceaux', Positif, 483 (May 2001), pp.29–30

Gorin, F. et J.-C. Loiseau (2001) 'Le Fabuleux destin d'Amélie Poulain', Télérama, 25 April 2001

Hémery, A. (2001) 'Alain Carsoux: Le Fabuleux destin d'Amélie Poulain', SFX, May–June 2001, pp.42–44

Jeunet, J.-P, (2001) Interview, Studio Magazine 166, May 2001, pp.98–105

Jeunet, J.-P., G. Laurant and P. Casoar, Le Fabuleux album d'Amélie Poulain (Paris: Editions Les Arènes, 2001)

Jeunet, J-P., G. Laurant and L. Desportes, Le Fabuleux destin d'Amélie Poulain, Collection storyboard (Paris: Alvisa, 2004)

Journot, M.-T., 'L'Esthétique publicitaire' dans le cinéma français des années 80 la modernité en crise (Paris: L'Harmattan, 2004)

Kaganski, S. (2001) 'Amélie pas jolie', *Libération*, 31 May 2001

Kaganski, S. (2001) 'Pourquoi je n'aime pas Le Fabuleux destin d'Amélie Poulain', *Inrockuptibles*, 31 May 2001

Kempley, R. (2001) 'Amelie: candy-coated, magically delicious', *Washington Post*, 9 November 2001, p.5

Lalanne, J.-M. and D. Péron (2001a) 'Un bonheur indescriptible à fabriquer', *Libération*, 25 April 2001

Lalanne, J.-M. and D. Péron (2001b) 'Un coup de Jeunet', *Libération*, 25 April 2001

Lamome, S. (2001) 'Jeunet joli', *Première* 290, May 2001

Lançon, P. (2001) 'Le frauduleux destin d'Amélie Poulain', *Libération*, 1 June 2001

Larcher, J. (2001) 'Le Cabinet des curiosités', *Cahiers du cinéma*, May 2001, p.112

Lavoignat, J.-P. (2000) 'Le Paris de Jean-Pierre Jeunet', *Studio Magazine* 158 (July 2000), pp.12–17

Lavoignat, J.-P (2001a) 'Le Pacte magique', *Studio Magazine* 168, June 2001, p.5

Lavoignat, J.-P. (2001b) '2001 ou le triomphe du cinéma français', *Studio Magazine*, Hors Série 2001, pp.54–65

Lavoignat, J.-P. (2001c) 'Jean-Pierre Jeunet: ce qui m'arrive est exceptionnel', *Studio Magazine*, Hors Série 2001, pp.66–73

Lefort, G. and D. Péron (2001) 'Je ne suis pas prêt de revivre un tel miracle', *Libération*, 26 December 2001, p.21–22

Libiot, E., '*Le Fabuleux destin d'Amélie Poulain*' *Annuel du cinéma* (Paris: Fiches Cinéma, 2002), pp.624–630

Libiot, E. (2004) 'Le Musée imaginaire de Jean-Pierre Jeunet: que du cinéma', *Express*, 1 November 2004

Lichfield, J. (2001) 'French elite horrified as feel good film seduces nation', *Independent*, 2 June 2001, p.15

Marvier, M., 'Jean-Pierre Jeunet, le collectionneur: Interview de Jean-Pierre Jeunet', *Synopsis* 13, May–June 2001, pp.52–55

Meyer, A. (2001) 'The fabulous destiny of Jean-Pierre Jeunet', *Indiewire* World Wide web, http://www.indiewire.com/people/int_Jeunet_JeanPier_011102.html, accessed on 10 November 2003

Moine, R., 'Vieux genres? Nouveaux genres? Le fabuleux destin de quelques films français' in *Cinéma contemporain: état des lieux*, J.-P. Esquenazi ed., (Paris: L'Harmattan, Champs Visuels, 2004), pp. 151–166

Montebello, F., *Le Cinéma en France* (Paris: Armand Colin, 2005)

Moore, R.C. 'Ambivalence to technology in Jeunet's *Le Fabuleux destin d'Amélie Poulain*', *Bulletin of Science, Technology and Society* 26. 1 (February 2006), pp.9–19

Paumier, P. and E. Cirodde, 'Jean-Pierre Jeunet: Retour aux sources', *Ciné Live* 45 (May 2001)

Péron, D., 'Quatre millions d'adhérents au parti d'Amélie Poulain', *Libération*, 2 June 2001

Pliskin, F., 'D'Amélie à Pitof: Le Paris virtuel', *Nouvel Observateur*, 20 September 2001

Potton E., 'Gallic crush', *Times* 6 October 2001, p.7

Powrie, P., 'The fabulous destiny of the accordion in French cinema', in P. Powrie and R. Stilwell (eds), *Changing Tunes: The Use of Pre-existing Music in Film* (Aldershot: Ashgate, 2006), pp.137–151

Prédal, R., *Le Jeune Cinéma français* (Paris: Nathan, 2002)

Preston, P. 'Soft choux shuffle', *Guardian*, 7 October 2001

Pride, R. (2001) 'Magnificent obsession', *Filmmaker*, Autumn 2001, World Wide Web, http://www.filmmakermagazine>com/fall2001/features/magnificent_obsession.html, accessed on 14 November 2004

Priot, F., *Financement et devis des films français* (Paris: Dixit, 2005)

Quinn, A. (2001) 'The big picture: Amelie', *Independent*, 5 October 2001, p.10

Reumont, F. (2001) 'Le Destin de l'étalonnage numérique: Bruno Delbonnel, chef opérateur', *Technicien du film* 511 (May 2001), pp.25–28

Rolandeau, Y. (2002) 'Amélie Poulain: révélations et bonheur guimauve', *Hors Champ*, January 2002. World Wide Web site http://www.horschamp.qc.ca/article.php3?id_article=22, last accessed 4 January 2005

Rosello, M. 'Auto-portraits glanés et plaisirs partagés', *Esprit créateur* 42. 3 (2002), pp.3–17

Roux, B. (2001) 'Les vertiges de l'intimité', *Positif* 487, September 2001 pp.64–65

Rouyer, P. and C. Vassé (2004) 'Entretien Jean-Pierre Jeunet: dans une autre vie je suis mort à la guerre de 14', *Positif* 525 (November 2004), pp.8–12

Scatton-Tessier, M. 'Le Petisme: flirting with the sordid in *Le Fabuleux destin d'Amélie Poulain*', *Studies in French Cinema* 4. 3 (2004), pp.197–207

Séguret, O. 'Cannes, son délit d'Amélie', *Libération*, 9 May 2001

Sotinel, T. (2001a) 'Le Fabuleux destin d'Amélie Poulain: quand Georges Perec rencontre Marcel Carné', *Le Monde*, 24 April

Sotinel, T. (2001b) 'Amélie et la boîte aux fantasmes', *Le Monde*, 8 June 2001

Temple, M. and M. Witt (eds), *The French Cinema Book* (London: BFI, 2004)

Tirard, L. 'La Leçon de cinéma de Jean-Pierre Jeunet', *Studio Magazine*, Hors Série, (1997) pp.122–127

Tisseron, S. 'D'Amélie Poulain au Seigneur des anneaux: un désir de merveilleux', *Le Monde Diplomatique* (March 2002), pp.30–31

Tobias, S. 'Jean-Pierre Jeunet', *The Onion A.V. Club* 37. 39, 31 October 2001. World Wide Web http://avclub.theonion.com/avclub3739/bonusfeature1_3739.html, accessed on 24 September 2003

Turan, K. (2001) 'Mean streak hurts Amelie', *Los Angeles Times*, 2 November 2001

Vincendeau, G. 'Café society', *Sight and Sound* 11. 8 (August 2001), pp.22–25

Vincendeau, G. (2005) 'Miss France', *Sight and Sound* (February) pp.12-15. also available at http://www.bfi.org.uk/sightandsound/2001_08/cafesociety.html.

Voiturin, S. 'Amélie Poulain fabuleusement sublime', *Sonovision* 451 (May 2001), pp. 14–17

V. Walt (2001) 'Amelie features a real parisian neighborhood', *USA Today*, 11 February 2001

Waskiewicz, S. 'Le Fabuleux destin d'Amélie Poulain', *French Politics Culture and Society* 20. 1 (2002), pp.152–155

Internet sites

Jean-Pierre Jeunet official site:
http://www.jpjeunetlesite.online.fr
'*Le Fabuleux destin d'Amélie Poulain*'
http://www.zoomavant.com/dossier/02/ameliepoulain/introduction.htm

Index